DATE DUE

MAR 0 1 2007	
APR 1 0 2008	

DEMCO, INC. 38-2931

IN SO MANY WORDS

IN SO MANY WORDS

Arguments and Adventures

R O B E R T ■ S C H M U H L

University of Notre Dame Press   *Notre Dame, Indiana*

Manufactured in the United States of America

Library of Congress Cataloging-in-Publication Data

Schmuhl, Robert.
In so many words : arguments and adventures / Robert Schmuhl.
    p.   cm.
Includes bibliographical references.
ISBN-13: 978-0-268-04123-6 (cloth : alk. paper)
ISBN-10: 0-268-04123-7 (cloth : alk. paper)
1. United States–Politics and government. 2. Political culture—United States.
3. Journalism—United States. 4. American literature. 5. United States—
Civilization. I. Title.
JK21.S23   2006
306.20973—dc22

                                     2006018594

To John W. Gallivan

and

his family

for their values and vision

today and tomorrow

Contents

Part II. Matters Literary

III. Matters Personal

Acknowledgments

Many editors made this book possible by seeing potential merit in a writer's query or by assigning an article. Walt Collins, Kerry Temple, and Carol Schaal of Notre Dame Magazine were always open to ideas, and they improved each submission. Elizabeth Taylor, the literary editor of the Chicago Tribune, was encouraging and receptive to several essays that (it pains an author to admit) reduced the space for reviewing new titles in her "Books" section. I'm grateful to every editor with whom I worked and to the publications where these articles first appeared.

This is the sixth book of mine the University of Notre Dame Press has published. Sincere thanks to Barbara Hanrahan, the director; Rebecca De-Boer, the managing editor; John de Roo, the manuscript's copy editor; Lowell Francis in acquisitions; and everyone else at the press for helping to shape a tentative first proposal into a finished volume.

When Rev. Edmund P. Joyce, C.S.C, Notre Dame's longtime and legendary executive vice president, passed away in 2004, the Annenberg Foundation made a contribution to the university to honor Father Joyce and to recognize his involvement in Annenberg-related activities. A small portion of that generous gift is helping to support this publication.

This book is dedicated to John W. Gallivan and the Gallivan family. For several years, I've directed the John W. Gallivan Program in Journalism, Ethics & Democracy at Notre Dame. Gallivan generosity has provided a journalist-academic with the opportunity to help create a new, innovative approach to journalism education. I'm grateful to them, to the program's advisory committee, to the faculty, and to the students.

Mark Roche, dean of the College of Arts and Letters at Notre Dame, and Ben Giamo, chair of the university's Department of American Studies, have been enormously helpful as the Gallivan Program developed, and both recognize the significance and value of journalism as a pursuit and as a subject for study.

In preparing this manuscript, Lisa Yates and Cheryl Reed provided advice and assistance that resulted in the planned, sequential ordering of all the articles here.

With characteristic Southern charm, William Faulkner once remarked: "If a writer has to rob his mother, he will not hesitate; the Ode on a Grecian Urn is worth any number of old ladies." Said less memorably, stringing words together can be a selfish obsession, often conducted to the cruel exclusion of family and friends. In my case, Judith Roberts Schmuhl and our son, Michael, are loving (and lovable) enablers for a wayward wordsmith. They deserve an anthem or an ode instead of a brief paragraph of appreciation.

Introduction

Any book-length collection of previously published articles is—in a writer's wishful thinking—a search for literary longevity. Frequently composed on deadline and printed in an array of places, periodical pieces are often difficult to track down in bound volumes, on microfilm, or through online archives. Book publication provides ordered permanence and helps convey, justifiably or not, a sense of continuing pertinence for work originally appearing in here-today, gone-tomorrow newspapers and magazines. A collection's future might mean consignment to a library shelf somewhere, but even that fate offers comforting consolation. A decade or two from now, maybe some unsuspecting reader will find words assembled here either interesting or informative. One can always hope.

This volume is arranged thematically rather than chronologically, with the contents divided into three separate sections—Matters Political and Journalistic, Matters Literary, and Matters Personal. Each section begins with a brief, explanatory overview, setting the stage for what to expect. The arrangement, however, is somewhat arbitrary, with the book—and author—encouraging random perusal. You're at liberty to read from beginning to end—or haphazardly in any way you wish, even from front to back. Clustering is done for specific reasons, but there's no unfolding narrative (or plot) to pull you through the pages. Each effort stands on its own—leaving you, dear reader, on your own, too.

Most of the articles assembled here appeared during the last decade, although some favored ones from the more distant past seemed worth recovery and resuscitation. In all cases, either introductory headnotes or concluding postscripts contribute additional context to help understand a piece or a grouping of articles.

Besides providing explanations or up-to-date reflections in these transitional sections, I have taken the opportunity of new publishing life to touch up some sentences here and there along the way. Book publication affords a final (and welcome) chance to make a point with greater felicity—but in no case is the basic thrust or thinking behind an argument substantially changed. Topical references, rooting what's written in a particular time, remain intact as well.

A few offerings here are beneficiaries of other, related articles. When it was possible to strengthen a piece with a paragraph or two from another effort on the same topic, I didn't hesitate to do so. Most writers are, in their way, repetitive—frequently returning to certain themes or ideas—but each "take" includes a different approach or new material. Combining points for a book's final say does involve stealing from one's self, but that's not exactly a high crime or even a misdemeanor.

In a couple places, I restore words editors trimmed to accommodate a certain amount of space—to fill, in their lingo, "the available hole"—or revert to the phrasing originally submitted, if the final version was changed and I lost the battle of having what I composed, with timeliness a subordinate concern, appear instead of an editor's bias of wanting to chase that day's news. Losers rarely get the chance to write history, but a writer, if the case makes sense, usually gets the last word in a collection like this.

Some of the titles on the individual pieces are exactly as they were originally presented when first published. Others are new and more appropriate confections for their appearance within these pages.

According to dictionaries of idiomatic expressions, the phrase "in so many words" carries two meanings: precision or exactitude in language as well as candor or plain speaking. I hope the writing in this book lives up to its title. Moreover, the phrase has modest autobiographical resonance. For over four decades (starting at the age of fifteen), I've strung words together for publications large and small. I shudder to think at the number of trees no longer offering shade for "so many words" from one source.

The subtitle presented its own challenge. A survey of like-minded compilations usually turns up the single word "essays" or the somewhat more grandiose phrases "selected essays" or " collected essays." You also find the designation "reader" or "sampler" for such compilations. Settling on "Arguments and Adventures" attempts to vary prosy monotony and to abide by all truth-in-advertising laws. What you find here are, in the main, essays with their serious or playful arguments, yet there are other kinds of writing that seemed appropriate to include. Regardless of the narrative approach, each assignment presented its own compositional adventure, albeit for a mostly sedentary soul.

Despite the many years of seemingly incorrigible compulsion to set pencil to paper (alas, compositionally, I'm pre-Luddite in outlook and practice), the competing emotions of temerity and trepidation collide with any effort. Confidence, if not tempered bravado, in expressing one's views always wrestles with nagging fears a finished product might not (for some mysterious reason) meet with an editor's approval. Indeed, in full confessional mode, a couple articles here received editorial vetoes at first try but subsequently found proper homes at other places.

Auberon Waugh, the prolific British man of letters (and son of the even more productive and esteemed Evelyn Waugh) put the doubt that haunts a freelance scribbler in the title of his autobiography, *Will This Do?* As Waugh explains in his introductory "Apologia": "The only question left hanging in the air is the one which every journalist asks himself on submitting an article. It is also the one with which we may all eventually, in trembling hope, face our Maker: *Will this do?*" Eternity is well beyond our province here, but an earthly "trembling hope" is never far removed from these (or any other) jousts with language.

For a writer who's engaged in almost every form of publication—newspaper, magazine, academic journal, Internet website, and book—experience leads to rudimentary self-knowledge of genre preference. As with a participant on a track team, distance is defining. The literary sprinter enjoys the thousand-word dash, while the marathon wordsmith prefers—and often takes delight in—the book-length course.

I tend to favor shorter assignments rather than more daunting multiyear projects. However, in the back of my mind, I harbor the ego-propelled longing that some of the briefer pieces will ultimately live on between the covers of books. Several articles reprinted here have already found their way into other people's anthologies or textbooks. While advancing age and a catholicity of interests probably mean bygone days as a lonely, long-distance runner are over, this collection completes the thankful transformation of turning a stout-hearted (and stout-bodied) sprinter into a satisfied miler. The benevolent Maker and kind editors willing, there will be a good many more writing miles down the road in years to come.

PART I

Matters Political and Journalistic

Since 1975, my writing and teaching have focused on American political culture and contemporary communications, particularly the news media. What, you might ask, qualifies someone with a doctorate in English and American studies for such work? Well, back in '75 after a decade of part-time and freelance journalism and about half that time toiling off and on in politics and government, I was offered a job at an academic center, based at Indiana University (where I was in graduate school), that conducted programs in civic affairs and media analysis. I, in fact, coordinated one that was called "The Citizen and the News Project."

Five years later, when a faculty position in American studies opened up at the University of Notre Dame and they wanted someone to develop classes about the media and contemporary political life, I applied, got lucky, and began to stake out this relatively new territory by using a humanities-oriented approach. Except for an occasional course on American Humor, my background in literature, including a dissertation about Mark Twain, served as an apprenticeship for other academic pursuits. But I have no regrets. I moved out of literary studies just as vaporous theories began to float over the Atlantic to cloud the interpretive landscape, making me feel not only ill at ease but also out of place.

The articles that follow address—and assess—political and journalistic concerns. Most deal with current issues, but the last two look back to an earlier time. Since the 1980s, the work of Ben Hecht—a reporter to the core, despite a career with many other writing accomplishments—has been an abiding fascination. The Front Page, the classic play Hecht coauthored with Charles MacArthur, continues to shape how we view newspeople and what they do today.

Going Our Way: A New Foreign Policy

War is always a bloody interlude. Before the fury comes the triggering rationale—and afterward the consequences of scarring change.

The age-old pattern repeated itself last spring in Iraq. Beyond this theater of war, however, a related drama—with words as weapons—continues to play out nationally and throughout the world.

Is the policy that led the United States to take military action in the Persian Gulf based on defensive security or offensive superiority? Will America be measurably safer in years to come—or be more vulnerable to adversaries provoked by this new strategy?

Doubt and uncertainty followed the hostilities in Iraq for one prime reason. U.S. forces struck first in the campaign to remove Saddam Hussein and his government from power. Though assisted by British and Australian contingents, American might—dazzling in its high-tech sophistication, frightening in its earthbound execution—brought an end to savage despotism but did so without authorization by the United Nations or approval from many traditional U.S. allies. Moreover, the principal justification for war was itself something of a moving target. Eliminating weapons of mass destruction, preventing the development of nuclear armament capability, producing "regime change," and ending Iraqi assistance to terrorist organizations were among the reasons cited for combat before hostilities began.

Success, especially swift elimination of the tyrannous authority ruling Iraq, can obscure concern over the justification of military action. It shouldn't, though, because this use of force reflects a way of thinking and acting much greater in its international implications than the fate of one regime on its receiving end at a given time. How this policy took strategic shape before its first implementation tells a story about presidential decision making and our times that would have been difficult to foresee just two years ago.

For most of the 1990s and through the summer of 2001, domestic concerns preoccupied people in the United States. What was happening abroad merited only occasional media attention. International affairs played a minor role in the presidential elections of 1992, 1996, and 2000. When George W. Bush campaigned for the White House in 2000, he emphasized the virtue of humility in dealing with other countries and pointed out the dangers of nation building. In spring 2001, former secretary of state Henry A. Kissinger captured the prevailing national mood by asking a question as the title of a new book: *Does America Need a Foreign Policy?*

Everything changed on September 11, 2001. Zealots from distant lands turned commercial airplanes into makeshift missiles that killed more than three thousand people on U.S. soil. That evening Bush (in the presidency only seven months) called the response he envisioned a "war against terrorism" and vowed: "We will make no distinction between the terrorists who committed these acts and those who harbor them."

Nine days later, in an address to a joint session of Congress, the president amplified his thinking on the relationship between perpetrators of terror and countries abetting their malevolence. "We will starve terrorists of funding, turn them one against another, drive them from place to place, until there is no refuge or no rest," he said. "And we will pursue nations that provide aid or safe haven to terrorism. Every nation, in every region, now has a decision to make. Either you are with us, or you are with the terrorists. From this day forward, any nation that continues to harbor or support terrorism will be regarded by the United States as a hostile regime."

Although the explicit target for most of Bush's speech was Afghanistan and its terrorist-accommodating Taliban movement, the more encompassing words of warning suggested the possibility of a larger strategy. In retrospect, toppling the Taliban and destroying the terrorist training camps in Afghanistan—actions widely supported by the world community—served as a first step down a road that quickly took a sharp turn away from a definite goal.

The turn came on January 29, 2002, during the president's first State of the Union address. With the new leader of "liberated" Afghanistan—Hamid Karzai—in attendance, Bush praised "the might of the United States military," deployed seven thousand miles away, but he moved shortly thereafter to identify three countries never directly associated with September 11 that could at some point prove dangerous to "America or our friends and allies."

Branding North Korea, Iran, and Iraq "an axis of evil," he trained his rhetorical fire on the weaponry at their disposal and the risks they posed. In language both personal and provocative, the president went further than before in articulating a policy of direct action: "We'll be deliberate, yet time is not on our side. I will not wait on events, while dangers gather. I will not stand by, as peril draws closer and closer. The United States of America will not permit the world's most dangerous regimes to threaten us with the world's most destructive weapons."

Talk of an "axis of evil" now competed with "a war against terrorism," perplexing public thinking at home and abroad. The focus on tracking down those responsible for September 11 became blurred, with the president expanding on potential enemies as well as those currently in the crosshairs.

Why, people wondered, link these three countries—Iran and Iraq had fought a protracted war in the 1980s, while North Korea has long isolated itself from the rest of the world—in an unholy trinity of evil without immediate relevance to the military action under way in Afghanistan? Whether "hit list" or formal warning, the explicit connections among the trio lacked immediately identifiable coherence, furrowing brows at home and abroad.

Speaking at West Point graduation ceremonies on June 1, 2002, Bush built on his earlier statements to provide a more encompassing strategic framework for America's engagement in international affairs. Specific as to purpose without naming particular countries, he set forth what he called "new thinking" to confront "new threats."

Looking back to the Cold War, with its reliance on deterrence and containment to control the aggression and ambition of "imperial communism," the president pronounced those strategies anachronistic in a time of terrorism. "Deterrence—the promise of massive retaliation against nations—means nothing against shadowy terrorist networks with no nation or citizens to defend," he said. "Containment is not possible when unbalanced dictators with weapons of mass destruction can deliver those weapons on missiles or secretly provide them to terrorist allies."

With deterrence and containment no longer central tenets, Bush proposed a more direct approach: "We must take the battle to the enemy, disrupt his plans and confront the worst threats before they emerge. In the world we have entered, the only path to safety is the path of action. And this nation will act."

Shortly after asserting this general principle for dealing with perceived threats, the president became more precise about what he had in mind. Three consecutive sentences began with the phrase "Our security" and went on to advocate modernization in intelligence, domestic agencies (like the FBI), and the military. He concluded the passage with a more detailed and eye-opening statement: "And our security will require all Americans to be forward-looking and resolute, to be ready for preemptive action when necessary to defend our liberty and to defend our lives."

Surrounded by appeals for ensuring "our security" and defending "our liberty" and "our lives," the concept of preemptive action entered the arena of policy debate. In the eight months since September 11, Bush had used four major speeches to articulate an approach to international affairs that became less abstract and more assertive as his thinking and that of his administration evolved.

That approach served as the foundation-setting prelude to a formal, thirty-one-page document, "The National Security Strategy of the United States of America," which was issued September 20, 2002.

Much of the document's prose is predictable, championing human dignity, economic growth, and the development of democracy. What's striking, however, is the explicit rejection of the Cold War tactic of deterrence and the repeated emphasis on preemption as an option in dealing with potential dangers. Midway through the report required by Congress of every administration, September 11 is mentioned right before one reads these two paragraphs:

> The United States has long maintained the option of preemptive actions to counter a sufficient threat to our national security. The greater the threat, the greater is the risk of inaction—and the more

compelling the case for taking anticipatory action to defend ourselves, even if uncertainty remains as to the time and place of the enemy's attack. To forestall or prevent such hostile acts by our adversaries, the United States will, if necessary, act preemptively.

The United States will not use force in all cases to preempt emerging threats, nor should nations use preemption as a pretext for aggression. Yet in an age where the enemies of civilization openly and actively seek the world's most destructive technologies, the United States cannot remain idle while dangers gather.

Release of the official report spelled out in detail what's become known as the "Bush Doctrine." Despite diplomatic declamations about working with allies, friends, and international institutions to achieve common objectives, America served notice on the world that (in words at the end of the document) "we will be prepared to act apart when our interests and unique responsibilities require." By stressing preemption and suggesting unilateralism, the administration was positioning the nation to be robustly preeminent— and people here and in other countries started paying closer attention to what the United States might do.

To be sure, the American military had acted preemptively in the past— most recently in the Dominican Republic in 1965, in Grenada in 1983, and in Panama in 1989. But putting preemption at the center of a new strategic doctrine struck many observers as undue saberrattling by the world's only superpower—which in some circles abroad was increasingly identified as a "hyperpower," given its economic, military, technological, and cultural clout. By subordinating deterrence and stressing preemption, the United States was saying, in effect, we'll assess any outside threats and act accordingly, including the possible use of force.

Intriguingly, a decade earlier a draft proposal with thinking quite similar to that in "The National Security Strategy" document circulated during the final year of the first George Bush presidency—and was severely criticized within and outside the administration. Called the "Defense Planning Guidance" report, the forty-six-page plan discussed the option of preemptive action to maintain American primacy, regardless of the challenge from friend or foe.

Leaked to the *New York Times* and the lead story in its Sunday edition of March 8, 1992, the policy proposal received extensive treatment. The thrust of the argument is clear from a few sentences of the plan: "Our first objective is to prevent the re-emergence of a new rival, either on the territory of the former Soviet Union or elsewhere, that poses a threat on the order of that posed formerly by the Soviet Union. This is a dominant consideration underlying the new regional defense strategy and requires that we endeavor to prevent any hostile power from dominating a region whose resources would, under consolidated control, be sufficient to generate global power."

After specific areas—Western Europe, Eastern and Southwestern Asia, and the region of the former Soviet Union—are identified, the report elaborates on its principal objective and moves beyond defensive concerns:

> First, the U.S. must show the leadership necessary to establish and protect a new order that holds the promise of convincing potential competitors that they need not aspire to a greater role or pursue a more aggressive posture to protect their legitimate interests. Second, in the non-defense areas, we must account sufficiently for the interests of the advanced industrial nations to discourage them from challenging our leadership or seeking to overturn the established political and economic order. Finally, we must maintain the mechanisms for deterring potential competitors from even aspiring to a larger regional or global role.

Appearing as the 1992 presidential campaign was gathering momentum, the proposal for a regimen of unrivaled superiority was assailed by Patrick Buchanan, who was challenging Bush for the Republican nomination, and several Democratic contenders. More significantly, the plan received strong opposition inside the Bush administration. A follow-up article in the *New York Times* three days after the story first received attention reported: "One Administration official, familiar with the reaction of senior officials at the White House and State Department, characterized the document as a 'dumb report' that 'in no way or shape represents U.S. policy.'"

What's fascinating (and relevant) in looking back at this controversial report is its resemblance to the current security strategy and its conceptual parentage. At the time Dick Cheney was serving as secretary of defense, and

Paul Wolfowitz was the Pentagon's undersecretary for policy with responsibility for developing the plan. Today, of course, Cheney is vice president with a strong say in international affairs, and Wolfowitz is deputy secretary of defense and a principal architect of the nation's strategic thinking.

Through the Clinton administration years of the 1990s, Cheney, Wolfowitz, and other officials currently serving in government considered Iraq a nagging nemesis. Indeed, in 1998, the Project for the New American Century, a Washington policy center with ties to (among others) Cheney and Wolfowitz, issued an open letter to President Bill Clinton, summarizing the dangers of Saddam Hussein staying in power and calling for action.

"The only acceptable strategy is one that eliminates the possibility that Iraq will be able to use or threaten to use weapons of mass destruction," the letter stated. "In the near term, this means a willingness to undertake military action as diplomacy is clearly failing. In the long term, it means removing Saddam Hussein and his regime from power. That now needs to become the aim of American foreign policy."

Out of the eighteen signatories to the letter, ten later joined the Bush administration, including Secretary of Defense Donald Rumsfeld, Deputy Secretary of State Richard Armitage, and Wolfowitz. While toppling Saddam Hussein was a long-standing objective, there needed to be a triggering opportunity.

According to Bob Woodward's insider account, *Bush at War*, Rumsfeld and Wolfowitz raised the possibility of military action against Iraq immediately after the al Qaeda terrorist assaults on September 11, 2001. Worried about international reaction, Secretary of State Colin Powell argued against such thinking without direct evidence of Iraqi involvement.

As Bush subsequently told Woodward, "My theory is you've got to do something and do it well and that . . . if we could prove that we could be successful in [the Afghanistan] theater, then the rest of the task would be easier."

Iraq remained on the administration's radar screen as it considered larger security issues and threats in the post–September 11 world. Proposals (such as the thinking behind the decade-old Defense Department draft report) that previously seemed too radical, even unthinkable, now commanded attention. The post-9/11 environment, with its anxiety and fear, brought preemption and preeminence to the fore as core tenets of the Bush Doctrine.

Firing the first shot in Iraq seemed reasonable and appropriate to observers of differing viewpoints. Max Boot, a senior fellow at the Council on
Foreign Relations, argued in the New York Times, "It is certainly true that preemptive wars are not the norm in history. But they are not as rare as President
Bush's critics suggest. The president's preemption doctrine—and its first ap-
plication, in Iraq—is firmly rooted in centuries of tradition." After listing
several historical precedents, Boot asks: "[W]ho today thinks it was wise of
Britain and France to stay their hands in the 1930s when they could have
thwarted Hitler's ambitions early on?"

Journalist and commentator Christopher Hitchens, a self-described "con-
trarian" with intellectual roots in leftist ideology, stood foursquare for preemption in Iraq. Writing in his quickly published collection of "polemics"
favoring force, A Long Short War, he asserted: "If the Bush administration actually went around deposing all bad guys, as the peaceniks taunt it for not
doing, then that really would constitute preemption. But how preemptive is
an intervention in Iraq, when undertaken to enforce a multiply reaffirmed
resolution of international law? Saddam has been warned and put on notice
and the entire debate on armed enforcement has been exhaustively conducted in full public view."

Despite the sinister threat of global terrorism, the new policy impressed
many commentators as overly bellicose and individualistic. Harvard professor
Stanley Hoffmann criticized the assumption that "presumes that the United
States is the sole judge of the legitimacy of its own or anyone else's preemptive strikes." He went on to argue that "the Bush Doctrine proclaims the
emancipation of a colossus from international constraints (including from
the restraints that the United States itself enshrined in networks of international and regional organizations after World War II). In context, it amounts
to a doctrine of global domination."

The essayist Wendell Berry closely analyzed the text of "The National
Security Strategy" and observed: "This document affirms peace; it also affirms peace as the justification of war and war as the means of peace—and
thus perpetuates a hallowed absurdity. But implicit in its assertion of this
(and, by implication, any other) nation's right to act alone in its own interest
is an acceptance of war as a permanent condition. Either way, it is cynical to
invoke the ideas of cooperation, community, peace, freedom, justice, dignity,

and the rule of law (as this document repeatedly does), and then proceed to assert one's intention to act alone in making war."

Other analysts considered the new strategic approach as out of character with traditional American ideals and behavior, especially our historic reluctance to use the military except out of necessity. "There never was a good war or a bad peace," Benjamin Franklin wrote back in 1783, a statement frequently repeated in 2003. One commentator quoted former president and World War II Allied commander Dwight D. Eisenhower's opinion on preventative war: "I don't believe in such a thing, and frankly I wouldn't even listen seriously to anyone that came in and talked about such a thing." Another recalled the words of Eisenhower's White House successor, John Kennedy, who boldly asserted in the swelter of the Cold War: "The United States, as the world knows, will never start a war."

Times—and thinking—change. Behind any strategy of a first-strike option is the conviction that military force is required for self-defense in the face of an imminent threat. A targeted attack on a potential enemy, it is hoped, will remove likely peril to Americans here at home or abroad. To avoid another September 11, doesn't it make sense to do whatever's possible beforehand?

Yet, probed more deeply, the policy raises other questions that can't be ignored. Is the United States absolutely certain of its vulnerability in a given situation? Does the government, through its intelligence agencies, have proof-positive evidence of imminent danger? Has every other option to tame a threat been exhausted? Will going on the offensive prove to be the strongest defense to avoid greater and more protracted conflict? What harm might innocents face?

Such questions gained greater pertinence in the months following the major hostilities in Iraq, when evidence of weapons of mass destruction could not be found. A primary justification for waging war seemed suspect, and the administration's credibility came under fire domestically and internationally.

Just forty-eight hours before combat began, the president told the nation (and world): "Intelligence gathered by this and other governments leaves no doubt that the Iraq regime continues to possess and conceal some of the most lethal weapons ever devised. This regime has already used weapons of mass destruction against Iraq's neighbors and against Iraq's people."

Mentioning the regime's "deep hatred of America" and its assistance to terrorists (including al Qaeda), he elevates the fear factor to a domestic concern: "The danger is clear: using chemical, biological or, one day, nuclear weapons, obtained with the help of Iraq, the terrorists could fulfill their stated ambitions and kill thousands or hundreds of thousands of innocent people in our country, or any other."

The inability to locate these metaphorical smoking guns struck many observers as damaging to the more encompassing Bush Doctrine. Writing in late June of 2003, conservative columnist George F. Will claimed that preemption as "the core of the president's foreign policy" was "in jeopardy" without discovery of the often-cited weapons. He went on to make his case:

> To govern is to choose, almost always on the basis of very imperfect information. But preemption presupposes the ability to *know* things—to know about threats with a degree of certainty not requisite for decisions less momentous than those for waging war.
>
> Some say the war was justified even if WMD are not found nor their destruction explained, because the world is 'better off' without Saddam Hussein. Of course it is better off. But unless one is prepared to postulate a U.S. right, perhaps even a duty, to militarily dismantle any tyranny—on to Burma?—it is unacceptable to argue that Hussein's mass graves and torture chambers suffice as retrospective justification for preemptive war.

Those are pointed words, and time might ultimately prove them premature. Yet, without indisputable assurance that danger looms, any first strike could be interpreted as unwarranted aggression or intervention from an outsider. Moreover, once combat ceases, securing the peace and rebuilding a country or area follow. This chancy work needs to take place with coherence and care so that the forces feeding the original threats don't rekindle or take an ominously new shape.

Besides such pragmatic considerations, moral concerns weave themselves through the Bush Doctrine, as they always do in matters involving life and death. In this particular situation, philosophers and theologians who specialize in just-war theory make nuanced distinctions between preemption and preventive war.

According to ethicists, if an identified enemy poses an imminent and grave threat to a country, then a proportionate, preemptive attack possesses moral legitimacy on grounds of self-defense. By contrast, a preventive war involves less immediate danger—and provokes more ethical debate. In this case, a nation worries that another country at some point in the future could use force against it, with action now preventing possible conflict later.

Whether last spring's action in Iraq was preemption or prevention—or something in between—remains in dispute, depending on one's viewpoint and basis for judgment. Within America, fear that Iraqi-made weapons of mass destruction would fall into the hands of terrorists opposed to the United States made many people see the use of force as preemptive and, hence, justified. Beyond our shores, public opinion was more inclined to regard what happened more critically—and even skeptically.

Although the terrorist attacks of 9/11 produced sympathy and solidarity for the United States throughout the world—a headline September 12, 2001, in the French newspaper *Le Monde* vowed *"Nous Sommes Tous Americains"* (We Are All Americans)—those sentiments proved short-lived. As the administration's security policy received scrutiny and as talk about war in Iraq grew louder, reactions from abroad took on a sharply anti-American tone.

One statistical study, conducted by Pew Global Attitudes and released last June after the major phase of Iraqi combat, found that favorable opinion of the United States had fallen in fourteen of fifteen countries surveyed since 1999–2000. Positive response to America declined in Great Britain, Canada, and Italy, with dramatic downturns (and less than 50 percent favorability) in South Korea, Germany, France, Spain, Brazil, Morocco, Indonesia, Turkey, and Pakistan. In Indonesia, 15 percent had a positive opinion of the United States—down from 75 percent earlier. Morocco and Turkey also showed precipitous drops. The lone country registering an increase in regard was Nigeria, up to 61 percent from 46—but 72 percent of Nigerians surveyed worried "very" or "somewhat" about a military threat from the United States.

Polls offer snapshots in numbers. Monitoring the news media in other countries through the months preceding and during the war in Iraq allowed Americans a different vantage point, in words and pictures, for viewing the nation and the policy it was pursuing.

The coverage proved soberingly revealing. For instance, William Pfaff, a syndicated columnist for the *International Herald Tribune*, quoted "a very senior retired officer in the German Army" a few weeks before the war: "You Americans have been telling us for 60 years that we must never go to war. You have made the Germans pacifists. We have accepted that war is never a solution. We believe that even more because of our own history. Now you attack us because Germans are against this war."

Once the fighting began, the coverage turned even more fiercely negative in portraying what the United States was doing. Especially in Arab-based media but elsewhere as well, gruesome images, focusing on civilian casualties, dominated the pages of newspapers and television screens. With our news organizations focusing on the military's heroism and technological prowess, it often seemed as though American outlets and foreign ones were reporting on unrelated realities happening simultaneously in the same place.

Applause at home for battlefield advances was countered abroad with anxiety and anger. "The political, cultural and social point of reference that America has been, is now eclipsed in the eyes of billions of people," editorialized one European paper. "The overwhelming impression: an imperial power is doing what it wants, regardless of its friends and its foes."

How long such thinking might persist is anyone's guess. Yet, beyond public opinion, there are broader, more tangible consequences the recent hostilities could have on, say, the sales of American products, the attention paid to our popular culture, the safe travel of U.S. citizens abroad, and other international interaction.

What's clear, however, is that people outside the United States now view this country with greater suspicion as a result of the Bush Doctrine. To call the reaction of many foreigners "anti-Americanism" is misleading. The animus is closer to anti–American security policy or anti–Bush administration—but over time one fears a more generalized antipathy might metastasize. Should that happen, the U.S. leadership role in the world and our influence in several realms could suffer—with a policy intended for national security becoming one that isolates or even ostracizes.

The debate before, during, and after the major military activity in Iraq brought into the open America's new approach to potential threats. In the United States, the focus remained on the specific case—removal of a murderous dictator who ruled not only with an iron fist but also with singular regard for his own fate and fortune. For people in other countries, the more abstract principle of preemptive attack as a continuing policy option overshadowed the particular, with questions and qualms dominant.

Many foreigners wondered whether the ends (toppling a tyrant) justified the means (outside intervention without direct provocation). Asked more pointedly by some critics: Did the justification for war (the repeated allegations of Iraqi-made weapons of mass destruction and that country's friendly relations with terrorists) warrant the means that resulted in the ends?

Doubts dog the new doctrine for several reasons. America, long viewed as a beacon of hope and opportunity, is now seen as less predictable and more predisposed to use its unparalleled power in a unilateral, we-know-best way. That image exacerbates the animosity reflected in public opinion, testing (if not weakening) our position in international organizations and our alliances with traditional allies.

To carry this thinking to its more ominous conclusion: Countries that consider themselves possible targets of the United States could be inclined to seek advanced weaponry, triggering a new arms race of frightening dimension.

In an ironic twist of unintended consequence, weapons of mass destruction might proliferate in response to the American strategy that seeks their control. Then, of course (and most depressingly), another country could engage in a preemptive attack against a potential enemy, citing the precedent in Iraq and using the United States as an example of conflict resolution.

These darker implications and possibilities of the first-strike doctrine deserve consideration because as a policy for governmental action its effects radiate out on a global scale. Fear about what might happen domestically in one country ends up casting an ominous shadow across the world at large.

In his commencement address at West Point last year, President Bush said, "America has no empire to extend or utopia to establish. We wish for others only what we wish for ourselves—safety from violence, the rewards of liberty and the hope for a better life." These noble words reflect the nation's soul and heritage, but they run the risk of sounding hollow if a doctrine of preemption and preeminence leads the United States to flex its military muscle without the certain provocation from a clear and present danger.

—*Notre Dame Magazine,*
Autumn 2003

Postscript

Even if the U.S. military's role in Iraq had ended shortly after major combat ceased in 2003, the policy of preemption deserves continuing scrutiny and debate. When principal justifications for war—the threat from weapons of mass destruction and Iraq's direct involvement with al Qaeda—don't turn out to exist, details discredit doctrine, and after-the-fact reasons come into being to provide a new rationale. In this case, removing a tyrant from power and promoting democracy in the Persian Gulf region moved to the fore with constant repetition.

This essay, which appeared as the cover story in the autumn 2003 issue of *Notre Dame Magazine*, provoked strong reactions. One letter to the editor began: "The best and most important article I have ever read in my alma mater's alumni magazine is the article 'Going Our Way' by Robert Schmuhl. I congratulate you for publishing this honest and factual analysis of the tragic situation President Bush has created for this country and the world by attacking, and then badly mishandling the situation, in Iraq." Another in its entirety read: "Professor Schmuhl's implicit defense of the wicked regime of Saddam Hussein, and his sympathy for Arab terror, is abhorrent and despicable. His evil brings shame to American scholarship and to the University. He should burn in hell for eternity for the terrorism he advocates." There seemed to be no middle ground in the responses, a reflection perhaps of our politically polarized times.

As I write now in 2005, over two years since America sent troops into Iraq, U.S. public opinion approving our policy and actions keeps declining. Getting out is proving much more difficult than getting in. And then, of course, there's the continued loss of life and injuries, both physical and psychological, for the American military, Iraqi forces, and innocent noncombatants.

At the beginning of 2005, Timothy Garton Ash, the Oxford University historian of the present and senior fellow at Stanford University's Hoover Institution, wrote: "With [George W.] Bush's latest funding request, I make the total cost of war and occupation more than $250 billion. How many lives around the world could have been saved for $250 billion?" That question takes on greater meaning as the financial—and human—cost keeps mounting to levels never envisaged in early 2003.

HEADNOTE

While the previous essay deals with the foreign policy of one president, the next five articles take up the presidency itself and campaigning for the White House. The first analyzes the paradox of presidential power, especially in recent years. Institutional elasticity, based on historical circumstances, results in periods of either expansion or contraction, with perils increasing when a president is challenged by members from other branches of government, by the news media, or by interest groups.

Possibilities and perils notwithstanding, running for the White House remains the ultimate ambition of just about every public figure who reaches a certain level of national political visibility. For instance, since John F. Kennedy, a senator from Massachusetts, narrowly defeated then vice president Richard Nixon in 1960, some fifty-five members of Congress (the vast majority from the Senate) have sought the nation's highest office. All lost, leaving Kennedy and Warren G. Harding in 1920 the only candidates ever to go directly from the Senate to the presidency. Earlier, James Garfield moved from the House of Representatives to the White House in 1881. That all three died in office, two at the hands of assassins, is less significant than the lesson that Americans are reluctant to elect legislators as decision-making executives and commanders in chief. Being victorious in a presidential campaign is just the first step down a treacherous road, as our recent history shows.

The four articles following the first one address some electoral subjects—the need to reform the nominating process, the changing nature of campaign narratives, the importance of televised debates, and what's shaping up to be a potentially distinctive race in 2008.

Power, Peril, and the Presidency

"Since 1792, the White House has become symbolic of the American presidency throughout the world," reads the sign greeting visitors to 1600 Pennsylvania Avenue in Washington, D.C. "While the Capitol represents the freedom and ideals of the Nation, the White House stands for the power and statesmanship of the chief executive."

Today, though, when you look around at what the sign refers to as "the most famous address in the United States," myriad security measures—heavily armed guards, bomb-sniffing dogs, huge concrete barriers—make the mansion resemble a modern-day fortress. At the same time the White House symbolizes presidential power, it is also readily apparent that danger and peril exist for any occupant of the Oval Office.

Back in 1797, while serving as vice president under John Adams, Thomas Jefferson observed in a letter: "The second office of this government is honorable & easy, the first is but a splendid misery." While the splendor of the presidency has grown during the past two centuries, so, too, has the potential for misery, especially in recent years.

Since 1961 (and not counting George W. Bush, who hasn't completed his second term at this writing), eight individuals, four Democrats and four Republicans, have served in the nation's highest office. Along with winning the Cold War, fostering prosperity at home, promoting democracy and free markets around the world, exploring space, and other achievements, history's scorecard records that three of the eight (Gerald Ford, Jimmy Carter, and

George Herbert Walker Bush) lost campaigns to remain in office, one (Lyndon Johnson) chose not to seek re-election fearing defeat, one (John Kennedy) was assassinated, one (Richard Nixon) resigned in disgrace to avoid impeachment and the possibility of removal from office, and one (Bill Clinton) was impeached by the House of Representatives but acquitted by the Senate. Ronald Reagan left the White House with his sunny disposition intact, yet he had to overcome an assassination attempt and the serious political wounds resulting from the Iran-Contra affair.

Why of late have there been so many difficulties in retaining presidential power? Why so many potentially crippling or even fatal challenges?

During Dwight Eisenhower's time in the White House, the political scientist Clinton Rossiter declared in his classic study *The American Presidency* (1956) that

> the President is not a Gulliver immobilized by ten thousand tiny cords, nor even a Prometheus chained to a rock of frustration. He is, rather, a kind of magnificent lion who can roam widely and do great deeds so long as he does not try to break loose from his broad reservation. Our pluralistic system of restraints is designed to keep him from going out of bounds, not to paralyze him in the field that has been reserved for his use. He will feel few checks upon his power if he uses that power as he should. This may well be the final definition of the strong and successful President: the one who knows just how far he can go in the direction he wants to go. If he cannot judge the limits of his power, he cannot call upon its strength. If he cannot sense the possible, he will exhaust himself attempting the impossible.

Seventeen years later, historian Arthur M. Schlesinger Jr. described the danger that can come from a lion on the loose or, in his phrase, a "runaway presidency" in his book *The Imperial Presidency*. Deploring "the expansion and abuse of presidential power," Schlesinger's book appeared as the Vietnam War was winding down and as the Watergate scandal was unfolding.

With a certain historical symmetry, Vietnam and Watergate raised questions and concerns over the concentration of power in the presidency, which had grown and strengthened as a consequence of two earlier national trials: the Great Depression and World War II. What Schlesinger chronicled served as a cautionary statement and captured the thinking of the time. Formal and informal measures quickly arose and broadened to serve as continuing checks on what a president might do.

The passage by Congress of the War Powers Act in 1973, the Budget and Impoundment Control Act in 1974, and the Independent Counsel Act in 1978 all served notice on the executive branch that other governmental entities outside the White House were monitoring the involvement of the military in hostile situations, the spending of appropriated funds, and the conduct of the presidents themselves and their appointed subordinates. (The Independent Counsel Act was not renewed in 1999, but by that time the administrations of Carter, Reagan, G. H. W. Bush, and Clinton had been vigorously investigated by an array of specially appointed prosecutors.)

Moreover, Supreme Court decisions (notably *United States v. Nixon* in 1974 and *Clinton v. Jones* in 1997) told presidents their standing in potentially criminal matters was the same as any other citizen. In the Nixon case, claims of executive privilege did not prevent surrender of his Oval Office tapes about Watergate. With Clinton, the argument of presidential immunity for an allegation of sexual harassment prior to taking office failed to delay court proceedings that involved Paula Corbin Jones and, ultimately, revealed to the world the name of Monica Lewinsky.

At the same time Congress and the Supreme Court were imposing checks on the presidency and individual presidents, the American news media were dramatically changing their approach and attitude to White House coverage. In the post-Watergate climate of unblinking scrutiny, a president always seemed under the media's microscope, a fact exacerbated by the ravenous appetite of a 24/7 news environment.

Gone were the reporter-as-stenographer days when Franklin Roosevelt could winkingly tell one of the 998 presidential press conferences he conducted in twelve years, "Where I am going I cannot tell you. When I am to get back I cannot tell you. And where I am going on my return I don't know. That's a lot of news, and it can't be released until I am ready."

As journalists became more probing and, at times, adversarial, previously taboo subjects (like a president's health or possible sex partners) became fair yet controversial game. Stories about Carter's near-exhaustion from jogging, Reagan's colon, Bush's reputed former mistress, and Clinton's acknowledged (and unacknowledged) extramarital activities circulated in ways testing limits of taste and privacy.

To illustrate the sea change in presidential reportage, it's worth remembering that in FDR's time reporters and photographers observed an unwritten pact to keep his inability to walk a secret and that revelations about affairs involving Kennedy and Johnson didn't become known until long after their presidencies. During the past quarter century, however, the line between what's public and what's private has blurred to the point of near invisibility, leaving journalists and citizens in a quandary about what's legitimate and what's out-of-bounds.

Aiding and abetting this tell all atmosphere about presidential matters is the loose-lipped coterie of White House officials and assistants who either leak anonymous, insider information to willing reporters or leave government service and write revealing, behind-closed-doors memoirs about presidents still in office.

Ever since Bob Woodward coauthored (with Carl Bernstein) *All the President's Men* and *The Final Days* about Nixon's misdeeds and eventual resignation, he has continued his fly-on-the-wall approach to the presidency in his reporting for the *Washington Post* and in a succession of best-selling books. His techniques have been widely copied in journalism and publishing, so that we now learn more than ever before about presidents in intimate settings neither scripted nor intended for public scrutiny. By gaining access to people in close proximity to Oval Office deliberations and decision making, this new breed of chronicler goes beyond the stagecraft and spincraft of contemporary statecraft, stripping away much of the mystery, not to mention majesty, of White House life.

For example, in Woodward's book *Shadow: Five Presidents and the Legacy of Watergate*, a reader learns about Clinton's split personality—openly warm and gregarious in public but either coldly calculating or given to temper tantrums away from the media lights. In addition, according to Woodward, the "small, windowless hallway" near the presidential study, where Clinton and Lewinsky got together, "was the only room in the White House which afforded him some privacy."

The argument could be made that any place of privacy is a site of temptation for some people, but the fact of having virtually no privacy in the whole

White House draws into question mythic notions of power. Clinton understood this early on, but it didn't inhibit him. Conducting a tour for an advisor
shortly after taking up residence at 1600 Pennsylvania Avenue, he remarked:
"Don't let it fool you. It's the crown jewel of the federal prison system."

Moreover and substantively, Woodward reports that Clinton even feared
taking notes at official meetings, lest the scribbling be subpoenaed for use in
court or by Congress. The potential historical value of having a record of
presidential thinking at a specific time is sacrificed because of apprehension
over possibly incriminating disclosure while in office.

Back in 1936, Franklin Roosevelt asked a committee of experts in public
administration to study how functions within the federal government could
improve. They recommended a larger presidential staff, which (in the words
of the committee) "should be possessed of high competence, great physical
vigor and a passion for anonymity."

In recent years, as the mania for celebrity has strangled any "passion for
anonymity" throughout American culture, many White House advisers have
become household names and later cashed in on their fame by writing tell-all
memoirs about their experiences. Even before Reagan completed his eight
years as president, publishers offered nearly a dozen you-are-there accounts,
questioning his work habits, style of governance and the influence of an as-
trologer (friendly with Nancy Reagan) on his travel schedule. Clinton, too,
was the subject of several revealing, "insider" books, a trend that continued
with George W. Bush.

As Bush prepared to run for re-election in 2004, he had to contend with
less-than-flattering portrayals in former terrorism assistant Richard Clarke's
Against All Enemies and the reminiscences of embittered treasury secretary
Paul O'Neill in the book *The Price of Loyalty*. Author Ron Suskind is specific
in describing O'Neill's reactions, noting at one point: "O'Neill was watching
Bush closely. He threw out a few general phrases, a few nods, but there was
virtually no engagement. These cabinet secretaries had worked for over a
month on detailed reports. O'Neill had been made to understand by various
colleagues in the White House that the President should not be expected to
read reports. In his personal experience, the President didn't even appear to
have read the short memos he sent over."

One paragraph later, Suskind quotes O'Neill directly: "'This meeting
was like many of the meetings I would go to over the course of two years,' he

recalled. 'The only way I can describe it is that, well, the President is like a blind man in a roomful of deaf people. There is no discernible connection.'" Although O'Neill's image insults the sensory disabled, it is even more of an affront to his former boss.

In the eyes of a president, someone who has served as a coat-holder—or cabinet member—can quickly become a turncoat, if that person reports words or actions considered to be private in sessions involving the making of public policy. How can a president maintain a sense of trust and security among those closest to power when the possibility of unflattering revelation always exists?

Considered collectively, the governmental, journalistic, and cultural changes of the past three decades result in a presidency in bold contrast to its earlier institutional standing. Indeed, with the end of the Cold War and the breakup of the Soviet Union, scholars and pundits wrote reams of commentary about the "shrinking" and "post-imperial" presidency.

Although textbooks for civic classes continue to describe the president as a combination chief executive, head of state, commander in chief, principal diplomat, legislative agenda-setter, crisis manager, and party leader, all these roles have become more difficult since the 1970s, a situation Vice President Dick Cheney has tried to remedy since the Bush administration began in 2001.

Cheney, former chief of staff under Ford and secretary of defense for the elder Bush, said during a television interview early in the first term, "What we have seen over the past 30 years is a continual encroachment by Congress in the executive branch, a weakening of the presidency. The president and I are bound and determined not to allow that to happen on our watch."

Later, interviewed by Woodward prior to the start of Bush's second term, Cheney, a House member from 1979 to 1989, argued that congressional encroachment had ended and that "there has been over time a restoration, if you will, of the power and authority of the president." Despite the disputed nature of the 2000 election, the vice president explained that the Supreme Court's 5–4 ruling, which ended the Florida vote-recounting process, didn't impede the administration.

"Even after we went through all of that, he [President Bush] never wanted to allow, correctly, the closeness of our election to in any way diminish the power of the presidency, lead him to make a decision that he needed to somehow trim his sails, and be less than a fully authorized, if you will, commander in chief, leader of our government, president of the United States," Cheney noted. He, however, went on to say that in the current, post-Watergate climate he doesn't keep a diary, use e-mail, or write letters—to avoid any paper trail investigators might pursue.

To a degree, Bush and Cheney have been able to seek a restoration of power because they have served for most of their time with a Republican-controlled Congress and during a security-conscious period arising from the September 11, 2001, attacks. Committing the military to hostilities in Afghanistan and Iraq were just the most visible presidential decisions in the more encompassing international war on terror.

In *Democracy in America*, Alexis de Tocqueville pointed out in 1835 a fact of political life that remains prophetically pertinent: "It is generally in its relations with foreign powers that the executive power of a nation has the chance to display skill and strength. If the Union's existence were constantly menaced, and if its great interests were continually interwoven with those of other powerful nations, one would see the prestige of the executive growing, because of what was expected from it and of what it did."

Wartime tends to concentrate power in the executive branch, with the president the principal beneficiary. Schlesinger returns to the problems of institutional imbalance and accountability in a more recent book, *War and the American Presidency* (2004). Arguing that George W. Bush's "presidency is the most secretive administration since Nixon," he goes on to observe: "The impact of 9/11 and of the overhanging terrorist threat gives more power than ever to the imperial presidency and places the separation of powers ordained by the Constitution under unprecedented, and at times unbearable, strain."

However, even amid extraordinary times, there's the possibility of over-reacting—and over-reaching. The Supreme Court's 2004 decisions involving the incarceration of enemy combatants served notice on the White House that it can go too far in trying to reassert its power and authority. In one ruling, Justice Sandra Day O'Connor declared: ". . . a state of war is not a blank check for the president when it comes to the rights of the nation's citizens." Justice Antonin Scalia, usually a reliable supporter of the Bush administration, added: "The very core of liberty secured by our Anglo-Saxon system of separated powers has been freedom from indefinite imprisonment at the will of the executive."

By the Founders' design, the American system is—in political scientist Richard Neustadt's clarifying phrase—"separated institutions, sharing powers." How, precisely, those powers are shared among the separated institutions depends, in part, on specific judgments rendered at a given time about certain circumstances. Checks that lead to perceived balance come into play to keep power within acceptable limits of control.

Even the most cursory study of U.S. history teaches that nothing is less permanent and more unpredictable than presidential fortunes. George W. Bush, who watched his father plunge from stratospheric approval ratings in 1991 to re-election defeat in 1992, remarked in his acceptance speech at the 2004 Republican National Convention: "One thing I have learned about the presidency is that whatever shortcomings you have, people are going to notice them, and whatever strengths you have, you're going to need them."

In *The Imperial Presidency,* Schlesinger sketched out a design for presidential conduct when he wrote: "The answer to the runaway Presidency is not the messenger-boy Presidency. The American democracy must discover a middle ground between making the President a czar and making him a puppet. The problem is to devise means of reconciling a strong and purposeful Presidency with equally strong and purposeful forms of democratic control. Or, to put it succinctly, we need a strong Presidency—but a strong Presidency *within the Constitution.*"

Finding that middle ground—the vital center, if you will—is a tricky and continuing balancing act between principle and pragmatism, between domestic concerns and international affairs, between traditional practices and new initiatives, between statecraft and stagecraft, between governing and campaigning, between appealing to the public at large and wooing a partisan base, between transparency and secrecy, and so on.

Time, too, is a critical factor. Presidents who win re-election have every reason to feel pride at the voters' ratification of their leadership, but second terms are notoriously difficult—as Nixon with Watergate, or Reagan with Iran-Contra, or Clinton with his impeachment imbroglio learned.

The confidence, if not hubris, that develops from multiyear presidential service collides with the stark reality of lame-duck status imposed by the two-term limit. An expiration date is stamped on the chief executive, and everyone—especially members of Congress facing their own re-election battles—know it all too well. In addition, a president's second term sets in motion the succession scramble, with potential candidates for the White House trying to show their own potential political muscle, often at the expense of the incumbent.

Not to put too fine a point on the current situation: If a candidate can endure the bruising gauntlet of a presidential campaign and triumph, then the victor confronts one or two terms in office resembling a tightrope walk across an abyss. The post-Vietnam, post-Watergate legislative reforms, certain Supreme Court decisions, the declining trust in politics, the chaos (and cost) of gaining the White House, and the general coarsening and intrusiveness of the media culture all contribute to a presidency much different, in power and stature, from the more remote past.

Theodore Roosevelt once remarked that "if there is not the great occasion, you don't get the great statesman; if Lincoln had lived in times of peace, no one would know his name now." But it's important to remember that the nation's highest office is also the most resilient one. Savvy and strong occupants of the Oval Office can transform the nation's political climate through forceful personal leadership that recognizes the boundaries of their legitimate middle ground. The presidency today remains endlessly perilous—even more so than a few decades ago—but it is also offers enduring possibility and promise.

—*The Boston Sunday Globe*, January 2, 2000,
with new additions in 2005

Postscript

As Bill Clinton was concluding his second term and the 2000 campaign was beginning, I wrote a lengthy assessment of the modern-day presidency. The impulse for the piece was a somewhat impolitic question: What does a person win by prevailing in a race for the White House? The essay here incorporates much of the original article, which appeared in the "Focus" section of the *Boston Sunday Globe*, and I've also added some new sections to reflect George W. Bush's consequential first term. For anyone who occupies the office, the presidency continues to be a tricky tightrope walk across a dangerous abyss.

Primary Madness

It's just not fair . . . or representative . . . or democratic.

Back in 2000, a *Washington Post*–ABC News poll asked a national sampling of adults and a random selection of New Hampshire voters the same question: "Overall, how much do you feel you know about the candidates running for president?"

In the countrywide survey, 64 percent answered "just some/hardly anything" as opposed to 35 percent commenting "a great deal/a good amount."

New Hampshire respondents offered a decidedly different viewpoint. In the Granite State, more than two-thirds (68 percent) felt they knew "a great deal/a good amount," while 32 percent said "just some/hardly anything."

The contrasting opinions in the two survey samples speak volumes about the convoluted system currently in place for nominating presidential candidates. It's as though the campaign for the nation's highest office takes place simultaneously on two distinct radio frequencies. What's clear reception, with informative messages, for one New England state is largely crackling and meaningless static for America as a whole.

New Hampshire and Iowa, where the presidential party caucuses take place first, are beneficiaries of ardent attention from White House aspirants and their campaign organizations for a simple reason. They exert a stranglehold on the nominating process stronger than any maneuver Jesse Ventura ever tried in his pro wrestling career. For New Hampshire and Iowa, being first in the nominating process means getting the chance to listen to and question the candidates directly as well as receive continuous exposure to the advertising and news coverage of their campaigns.

Is it any wonder that people in New Hampshire are confident in what they know about who's running? If the same question were posed in Iowa, the results would no doubt be similar.

What's titanically troubling, however, is that neither New Hampshire nor Iowa is typical of America. In demographic terms, according to the 2000 edition of *The Almanac of American Politics*, New Hampshire is 98 percent white. One percent of the people there are Hispanic, with African-Americans, Asian-Americans, and American Indians collectively making up another 1 percent. In Iowa, whites make up 96.7 percent of the population, with African-Americans at 1.7 percent, Hispanics at 1.1 percent, and other groups below a single percent.

Nationally, the following breakdown exists: 12.1 percent African-American, 9 percent Hispanic, 2.9 percent Asian-American, and 0.8 percent American Indian, with the remainder (about 75 percent) classified as white.

The skewing of minority representation is just one dimension of the un-representative nature of New Hampshire and Iowa in playing such influential roles in the presidential selection process. According to the Census Bureau's *Statistical Abstract of the United States*, 75.2 percent of Americans now are considered urban residents, with 24.8 percent rural. In New Hampshire, 49 percent fall into the rural category (double the national count), while in Iowa the rural number stands at 39.4 percent.

The oft-quoted maxim that "all politics is local" takes on new meaning when you think of candidates for national office debating agriculture subsidies and the virtues of ethanol at the expense of concerns with more urban resonance and consequence.

What's happened since the 1970s could be called "Primary Paradox and Caucus Conundrum." A process, originally intended to foster democratic involvement and deliberation, is now an every-state-for-itself free-for-all that not only lacks time for extended evaluation but also denies everyone except voters in the early states a genuine say in picking presidential nominees.

A case study of worthy objectives gone awry, the current system reflects the continuing, unintended consequences of political reform enacted in the wake of the tumultuous 1968 Democratic National Convention in Chicago.

When Vice President Hubert Humphrey won his party's presidential nomination without participating in any of that year's fifteen primaries, calls to
open up the selection procedures reverberated throughout the country, influ-
encing Democrats and Republicans alike.

The wheeling and dealing done in smoke-filled rooms by political bosses
(to invoke familiar stereotypes) had been under increasing criticism at the
time, and television's rising influence in politics since the 1950s had dramatically reduced party discipline and power. In state after state, new party policies made the United States the first democracy in the world to have voters
themselves choose nominees as well as officeholders.

By 1980, some thirty-seven states had jumped on the primary band-
wagon. But the jerry-built apparatus for producing future presidents ended
up looking as though it had been designed by the cartoonist-engineer Rube
Goldberg in his most inspired state of maddening convolution. Varying rules
defying easy explanation applied in various states, and the hope of methodi-
cally judging aspirants to the White House seemed to diminish.

In *America in Search of Itself,* Theodore H. White's last book about the
making of presidents, he wrote of the 1980 primaries, "There was no longer
any way of making a simple generalization about how Americans chose their
candidates for the presidency. What was worse, no school, no textbook, no
course of instruction, could tell young Americans, who would soon be voting, how their system worked. And if we of the political press had to cram
such rules into our heads as we moved from state to state, each with two par-
ties, and each state differing—how could ordinary voters understand what
professional observers had such difficulty grasping?"

That was 1980. Today campaign chroniclers have to cope with over forty
primaries (some open, others closed; some winner-take-all, others propor-
tional representation) in a crazy-quilt pattern featuring quadrennial date-
changing.

As the current method has increasingly spun out of control, proposals for
a national primary, a series of regional primaries, and even national conventions that would produce candidates to compete in late-summer or early-fall
primaries have circulated—but never gotten beyond the talking stage.

To avoid any advantage for a particular state or region and involve the entire electorate in a methodical, evolving exercise, what might make the most
sense would be to divide the country into five ten-state regions.

Three of the regions could vote in the successive months of March, April, and May, with the final two regions casting ballots on a decisive day in June. The drawing of lots on New Year's Day—the year of an election—would establish the precise order for the regional voting and, as a consequence, reduce early campaigning in one area or key state that a rotating process might encourage.

Such an arrangement has the virtue of extending the time of learning about the candidates and instituting a sense of national fairness. In this plan, Iowa and New Hampshire will be no different from any other state. Moreover, having two regions involved at the end forces a candidate to broaden his or her appeal for the summer's nominating convention and the fall's general election.

Back in the nineteenth century, British writer Samuel Coleridge remarked: "Every reform, however necessary, will by weak minds be carried to an excess, that itself will need reforming." The post–1968 reforms have not only been carried to ludicrous excess but also to a point that makes citizens question our larger political system.

National legislation is the only remedy for an idiotic process White described as "the madness of a good idea run wild." Figuring out and implementing a more logical, representative, and comprehensible way of selecting presidents would take a large step in the direction of achieving more faith in the nation's government and American democracy, but to do it requires leadership and courage.

It would take political bravery of uncommon, character-built spine for someone seeking the White House to pronounce in Iowa, New Hampshire, and elsewhere what really needs to be said: "If elected, one of my first acts as president will be to propose an entirely new nominating system that plays no favorites and fairly reflects the wishes of all Americans."

—*Chicago Tribune*, January 5, 2000,
and August 1, 1999; *Boston
Sunday Globe*, May 26, 1996;
Philadelphia Inquirer, May 10,
1994

Postscript

Trying to get American voters to consider the lunacy of the current presidential nominating process has been a hobby-horse obsession of mine for many years. This article brings together—in one effusion—sections from four similar-but-separate attempts to bring the issue to the public's attention in the last decade. Three appeared as op-ed page columns (two in the *Chicago Tribune* and one in the *Philadelphia Inquirer,* while the fourth, with the historical background, was an extended treatment for the *Boston Sunday Globe.* At this writing (in January of 2006), the Democratic Party is contemplating changes for 2008. One of these years something consequential and necessary might happen, but I'm not holding my breath.

What Teddy White Wrought

Henry Adams, a descendant of two presidents and sage evaluator of several others, remarks in his classic autobiography (*The Education of Henry Adams*): "The progress of evolution from President Washington to President Grant was alone evidence to upset Darwin."

Although Adams was dilating on presidents themselves, a survey of campaign chronicles over the past four decades reveals another kind of devolution: a deepening distaste for our electoral process that raises persistent doubts and questions about the ways candidates try to win the White House. Instead of exercises in civic virtue, political contests in their reconstruction now resemble brass-knuckled brawls.

In fact, the first book to appear about last year's race is Dana Milbank's *Smashmouth: Two Years in the Gutter with Al Gore and George W. Bush—Notes from the 2000 Campaign Trail* (Basic Books). Two others due out soon feature these tough-minded titles: *Down and Dirty: The Plot to Steal the Presidency* (by Jake Tapper; Little, Brown) and *Divided We Stand: How Al Gore Beat George Bush and Lost the Presidency* (by Roger Simon; Crown).

Milbank, a correspondent for the *Washington Post*, introduces his quickly assembled collection of reportage by saying: "[T]he purpose of this book is to celebrate the virtues of good, solid, in-the-gutter campaigning. Such nasty, smashmouth politics are said by the goody-goodies to be destroying our democracy, alienating the electorate and suppressing voter participation. I believe the opposite is true: that nasty is nice on the campaign trail, that it's cool to be cruel."

Milbank's archly snide attitude conforms to the prevailing approach among many political writers. For them, looking down is the appropriate vantage point when viewing public figures. Given this perspective, Olympus often seems like a molehill, but "the gutter" is always below—and the chroniclers invariably above.

That point of view (and its influence on how readers see subjects treated) stands in marked contrast to the way Theodore H. White first portrayed presidential politics. In *The Making of the President 1960*, a sense of awe infuses the opening paragraphs and sets the tone for the dramatic story of John Kennedy's 100,000-vote win over Richard Nixon:

> On election day America is Republican until five or six in the evening. It is in the last few hours of the day that working people and their families vote, on their way home from work or after supper; it is then, at evening, that America goes Democratic if it goes Democratic at all. All of this is invisible, for it is the essence of the act that as it happens it is a mystery in which millions of people each fit one fragment of a total secret together, none of them knowing the shape of the whole.
>
> What results from the fitting together of these secrets is, of course, the most awesome transfer of power in the world—the power to marshal and mobilize, the power to send men to kill or be killed, the power to tax and destroy, the power to create and the responsibility to do so, the power to guide and the responsibility to heal—all committed into the hands of one man. Heroes and philosophers, brave men and vile, have since Rome and Athens tried to make this particular manner of transfer of power work effectively; no people has succeeded at it better, or over a longer period of time, than the Americans.

The popularity of White's insider saga reflected a previously unknown public appetite for campaign books, and White delivered three sequels, about the races of 1964, 1968, and 1972.

As interest in presidential politics grew, competition among publishers developed for other works taking approaches different from White's start-to-finish recital of a campaign's progress. Joe McGinniss's *The Selling of the President 1968* exposed the Nixon campaign's adroit, manipulative usage of TV advertising to defeat Hubert Humphrey, and Timothy Crouse's *The Boys on the Bus* vividly rendered the involvement of print and broadcast journalists in what the public learned (or failed to learn) in the 1972 contest between Nixon and George McGovern. McGinniss and Crouse brought the media to center stage in presidential electioneering, a theme other writers exploited in accounts of subsequent campaigns.

In *The Boys on the Bus*, Crouse even devotes a chapter to Watergate, the illegalities and dirty tricks that took place in 1972 and eventually resulted in Nixon's resignation two years later. But as Crouse observes, "the Watergate affair failed to 'sink in'; its sinister implications never registered on the public's imagination. A Gallup poll taken around the time of the election found that 48 percent of the American public had never heard of the Watergate affair, and most of the rest didn't care about it."

One person who did care was Theodore White, who switched gears and wrote about the unmaking of a president in *Breach of Faith: The Fall of Richard Nixon*, which appeared in 1975. Seven years later—and in a more reflective than reportorial frame of mind—he produced *America in Search of Itself: The Making of the President 1956–1980*. A recurring theme of this summary work is that our electoral process has gone off the tracks with its emphasis on an inane nominating process and undue absorption in media-oriented theatrics.

Interestingly, when White died in 1986, obituaries noted that he'd come to "sincerely regret" the method of insider reporting in politics he pioneered. By that time so many writers were seeking access to behind-the-scenes maneuvering that those activities, too, were being choreographed to project specific images.

White's reservations about the state of campaigning and the book-length narratives following campaigns didn't stop others from trying their hand at this hybrid form of journalism and history. Most notably, veteran political reporter Jules Witcover spent more than two decades tracking White House candidates, sizing up the winners and losers.

Witcover described the rise of Jimmy Carter in *Marathon: The Pursuit of the Presidency, 1972–1976*. For his next four campaign accounts, Witcover collaborated with Jack W. Germond, who'd become his partner in a syndicated newspaper column.

The titles of their four books capture the spirit of each campaign and also echo White's doubts about the downward course of the American political process: *Blue Smoke and Mirrors: How Reagan Won and Why Carter Lost the Election of 1980; Wake Us When It's Over: Presidential Politics of 1984; Whose Broad Stripes and Bright Stars? The Trivial Pursuit of the Presidency, 1988;* and *Mad as Hell: Revolt at the Ballot Box, 1992.*

Witcover and Germond took a pass on the yawn-provoking 1996 contest between Bill Clinton and Bob Dole, but each writer weighed in with a book during 1999 to set the stage for the 2000 race. Witcover's *No Way to Pick a President* is a chapter-and-verse critique of the current system, while Germond's *Fat Man in a Middle Seat: Forty Years of Covering Politics* is a wry, eye-opening memoir that finds much greater fault with contemporary political life than what was happening a few decades ago.

Although White, Witcover, and Germond are not alone in objecting to the existing process, the vast sums of money it requires, and the centrality of image projection over substantive concerns, writers keep returning to presidential campaigns like gawkers to a traffic accident.

In 1992, Richard Ben Cramer sent many a head shaking with *What It Takes: The Way to the White House,* a 1,047-page opus that tracked some (but not all) of the candidates who'd run for president in 1988. An idiosyncratic epic, Cramer's novelistic rendering focused on the backgrounds of George Bush, Bob Dole, Michael Dukakis, Gary Hart, and others to such an extent that the fall campaign receives only passing mention in a tacked-on epilogue. In 1995, Cramer was able to fashion a separate book about Dole, the 1996 Republican hopeful, from the biographical chapters about him in *What It Takes.*

Former Chicago columnist (and current *U.S. News and World Report* correspondent) Roger Simon is the newest regular on the campaign-book beat. Besides his forthcoming account about the 2000 nail-biter, he looked behind the histrionics of the 1988 and 1996 contests in *Road Show* and *Show Time.* Simon's title for his book about 1996 comes from a refrain Clinton repeated whenever he left *Air Force One* for a campaign performance: "[H]e would square his shoulders, suck in his gut, turn to Harold Ickes, his deputy chief of staff, and say, 'Okay. Show time!'"

And, to be sure, the political show keeps going on, as candidates seek votes and writers seek readers for election-year sagas. At last count, more than a dozen books about the 2000 race and Florida recount will occupy shelf space before the end of the year.

Yet despite the volume of media coverage Bush, Gore, and their organizations received before and after Election Day, the central concerns today remain similar to those White wrestled with in *The Making of the President 1960*. What facts about a just-completed White House campaign deserve an afterlife for the sake of posterity, and how can the rendering of that information help us better understand American politics and history?

—*Chicago Tribune*, March 25, 2001

Postscript

In the wake of the 2004 presidential campaign between George W. Bush and John Kerry, one of the first extended looks back wasn't a book but a three-disc DVD collection. Comedy Central's *The Daily Show with Jon Stewart* produced "Indecision 2004," a compilation of mock (and mocking) reports and interviews. In one review, the *New York Times* noted, "The fake coverage of 'The Daily Show' often came closer to the truth than any real broadcast. And it is still very funny." "Indecision 2004" even won a prestigious George Foster Peabody Award. The distance between what Teddy White inaugurated and what now appears continues to grow.

The Living-Room Factor

When television became the principal tool for political communication, seekers of the presidency confronted a new challenge: they had to present themselves not only as plausible leaders of a world superpower, but also as visitors Americans would welcome in their homes.

Television made White House aspirants guests—invited or not—in our households, and they began dropping by at all hours. Between news reports, interview programs, talk shows, chats with late-night comics, and commercials, candidates are now unavoidable as they occupy our screens and seek our support.

Back in 1969, writer Michael J. Arlen called Vietnam the "living-room war." Today, because of television, the "living-room factor" plays an increasingly significant role in presidential politics. To a certain degree, the road to 1600 Pennsylvania Avenue goes through your residence.

Textbooks might describe national campaigns as contests of ideas, competing policies, and proposals charting the country's future. But those messages, by and large, come to us via our TV sets from candidates as concerned with how they dramatize themselves and their cause as with any wonkish prospectus or twelve-point plan.

The "living-room factor" means someone campaigning for president needs to conform to the medium's theatrical values. Portraying oneself as a comfortably likable person is essential. Television creates a sense of intimacy between candidate and voter, and the political figure hopes to become a regular guest in the collective American household for the campaign season—and the next four years.

The trick in cultivating a successfully telegenic "image" involves marrying personal traits—the authentic self—with qualities that make one engaging or appealing. If a candidate seems to a viewer to be in command and wears well, an emotional connection develops, and that bond can prove significant in the voting booth.

Before television, Franklin Roosevelt's mastery of radio in his "fireside chats" staked out the living room as a place politicians could go to establish a direct rapport with the citizenry. The nation listened, and FDR gave voice, authoritatively and compassionately, to problems Americans faced in their lives and homes.

With its visual dimension, television magnifies the connection radio created. An early observer of TV's growing involvement in political affairs was author Joe McGinniss. In his still-instructive account, *The Selling of the President 1968*, McGinniss chronicles how communication advisers to Richard Nixon transformed the former vice president, who had lost in 1960 to TV-savvy John Kennedy, into an image-oriented winner eight years later. Nixon's opponent, Vice President Hubert Humphrey, never found his footing on the new terrain of the political-media landscape.

"Television did great harm to Hubert Humphrey," McGinniss noted. "His excesses—talking too long and too fervently, which were merely annoying in an auditorium—became lethal in a television studio. The performer must talk to one person at a time. He is brought into the living room. He is a guest. It is improper for him to shout."

As television expands with more channels and means of delivery, chances for candidates to pop up—and pop by—multiply. It's no coincidence that since 1980, the only presidents to be elected twice—Ronald Reagan and Bill Clinton—used television so effectively that even opponents had to acknowledge their skill.

Reagan could poke fun at himself, but he understood what mattered. Leaving the White House, he told an interviewer: "For years, I've heard the question: 'How could an actor be president?' I've sometimes wondered how you could be president and not be an actor."

Although George W. Bush and John Kerry seem inescapable on TV these days, the upcoming debates provide sustained comparison. Especially for undecided voters, the living room will become a critical precinct for taking the measure of each candidate. At its heart, the viewer's decision is deeply personal: Do I agree with what animates or drives each nominee? Which one seems more genuine and convincing? Whom am I most comfortable with as a national leader in troubling times?

Four years ago during the debates, historian Richard Norton Smith remarked (on TV), "There is a dynamic in this race right now and it can be summed up by the question of whether you want Al Gore in your living room for the next four years or whether you want George Bush in the Oval Office for the next four years."

Behind Smith's sage quip were concerns about Gore's stiff, know-it-all persona and a perception that Bush, though likable, lacked high-office gravitas. Resolving that dilemma—and the race itself—proved anything but simple in 2000.

But there's also a larger point. Winning the Oval Office can depend on how well candidates come across in our living rooms—and whether we want to keep welcoming them into our homes.

—*Christian Science Monitor*, September 30, 2004

Postscript

Although a preview column, published by the *Christian Science Monitor* right before the three presidential debates of 2004, this essay is also a more general consideration of the role of television in contemporary campaigning for the White House. Someone (a sensitive copy editor probably) deleted the last sentence of the McGinniss quotation from *The Selling of the President 1968*: "Humphrey vomited on the rug." That image, vivid in its repulsiveness, leaves no doubt about the meaning of "the living-room factor" and its significance.

Debates offer the nation an extended last look at those who would be president and vice president. With their regularity since 1976, they have become something of a political and media yardstick for measuring the candidates that goes beyond a slogan, a ten-second sound bite, or a half-minute spot.

Do we make too much of the debates as testings for those seeking to govern America? Are rhetorical and dramatic skills unduly emphasized? Harry Truman once remarked: "I sit here all day trying to persuade people to do the things they ought to have enough sense to do without my persuading them. . . . That's all the powers of the president amount to." The power to persuade the public through effective use of television *is* a significant factor to successful leadership today. And (I firmly believe) any campaign organization that accepts federal funding for a presidential race should be required to participate in a series of debates the citizenry can watch and evaluate.

Getting Ready for 2008

As White House aspirants and aficionados of presidential politics look ahead to November 4, 2008, they'll see (however dimly) an Election Day different from any since 1952. If George W. Bush and Dick Cheney complete their second term—and the vice president keeps his promise not to make his own Oval Office run—the next national campaign will be the first in fifty-six years without either an incumbent president or vice president at the top of a major party ticket.

Incumbency doesn't dictate the winner of a presidential contest, as three presidents (Gerald Ford, Jimmy Carter, and George H. W. Bush) and three sitting vice presidents (Richard Nixon, Hubert Humphrey, and Al Gore) learned in six of the thirteen elections between 1956 and 2004. Yet occupying high office provides institutional advantages for campaigning and usually reduces intra-party challengers—the insurgent efforts of Ronald Reagan against Ford in 1976 and Senator Edward M. Kennedy's attempt to derail Carter in 1980 notwithstanding.

But continuity has been a hallmark for more than a half century, making the political landscape for 2008 largely uncharted territory. When Harry Truman decided not to seek a second full term as president in 1952, he opened the door for Illinois governor Adlai E. Stevenson and the first of his two unsuccessful races against World War II hero Dwight D. Eisenhower.

By choosing retirement over another campaign, Truman followed the practice of the two previous twentieth-century vice presidents who reached the White House because a president had either died or been assassinated. Both Theodore Roosevelt and Calvin Coolidge won individual terms on their own—but elected not to run again (in 1908 and 1928, respectively).

The fourth presidential campaign of the twenty-five between 1908 and 2004 without an incumbent president or vice president as Democratic or Republican standard-bearer took place in 1920. Warren Harding, the first senator to go directly to the White House (the only other was John F. Kennedy), defeated Ohio governor John M. Cox.

That the '52 battle between Eisenhower and Stevenson is the only non-incumbent contest over eight decades from 1928 to 2008 is, in part, a reflection of Franklin Roosevelt's democratic (and Democratic) dominion for a dozen years and, more recently, the elevation of the vice presidency to an office of governmental and political consequence.

The nation's first vice president, John Adams, confided to wife Abigail in a letter that he occupied "the most insignificant office that ever the invention of man contrived or his imagination conceived." Over a century later, John Nance Garner, FDR's running mate in 1932 and 1936 (before, unsuccessfully, seeking the presidential nomination against his boss in 1940), characterized the second spot as not "worth a pitcher of warm spit" (or words to that effect). But times and responsibilities change.

Beginning with Walter Mondale's policy involvement under Carter and especially with Cheney's influential clout throughout the current administration, vice presidents (who, constitutionally, act as president of the Senate) now do more than cast the occasional tie-breaking senatorial vote or serve as "stand-by equipment" in case something happens to the president.

During recent decades and in stark contrast to historical precedent, being number two has become a serious stepping-stone in seeking the highest office. In fact, assuming Cheney completes his second term and declines to run, he'll be the only elected vice president in well over a half century to end his allotted time as understudy without seeking the principal role. Even Truman's vice president, Alben Barkley, sought the Democratic nomination in 1952, but he received little support.

After Nixon lost to Kennedy in 1960, he came back in 1968 to defeat Lyndon Johnson's vice president, Hubert Humphrey. Mondale lost to Reagan in 1984, while Reagan's vice president, George H. W. Bush, won the presidency in 1988. Dan Quayle, Bush's veep, sought the 2000 Republican presidential nomination but couldn't stop George W. Bush, the winner over Bill Clinton's vice president, Gore. (Spiro Agnew, of course, was elected twice as, in the popular phrase, "Nixon's Nixon," but he resigned in disgrace in 1973, never returning to elective politics.)

It's possible, for whatever reason, Cheney will step down, permitting President Bush to select a new vice president, who could then run as an incumbent. Yet, barring health problems, this seems unlikely and would create the animosity of unelected favoritism within GOP ranks.

At this point, the election of 2008 is shaping up as the combination of an open-field marathon and an elbows-flying free-for-all. One website already lists nearly forty potential candidates in each party as possible contenders for the Democratic and Republican nominations. Will the next four years be long enough for Americans to make up their minds?

—*Chicago Sun-Times*, December 10, 2004

Postscript

By not having a designated and known heir as vice president, George W. Bush is less attuned to the politics of policies and proposals. Someone close to him, with monumental self-interest about the future, isn't able to argue (one way or another) about longer-term electoral implications of initiatives and decisions. The more isolated a presidency, the less inclusive a democracy.

HEADNOTE

The two essays that follow examine the American news media. Both appeared in *Notre Dame Magazine*, the first in the winter issue of 2002 and the second in the summer of 2005. The time that elapsed between the articles isn't particularly long, but in terms of the subject and the public's attitudes about contemporary journalism it seems like light-years.

"The Communal Lifeline" looks at media performance and coverage in the aftermath of the terrorist attacks of September 11, 2001. A collective sense that the seriousness of the time needed mirroring in the media's messages provided a refreshing responsibility veteran newspeople and their observers had been advocating for years. Praise and respect replaced criticism and disapproval post-9/11.

Unfortunately, in relatively short order, the mainstream sources of journalism returned to *status quo ante*. "News without End" focuses on the current mediascape, with the rise of alternative information forms a prominent feature—and source of concern. With so many messages competing for our attention, are we better informed about America and the world, or does a state of news overload make it more difficult to interpret what we as citizens really need to know?

The Communal Lifeline

In the dazed days following the atrocities of September 11, analysts and academics tried to come to terms with the unspeakable acts by speculating on their consequences. Such unprecedented terrorism created (in what began as a refrain and then became a cliché) a turning point, with potential for transforming America in ways large and small.

Nowhere was change more immediately noticeable than the response of the news media to the attacks and their aftermath. At a time of dwindling audiences, reduced budgets, and questionable practices, journalism approached the horror and heroism of a story like no other with a professionalism that critics—and citizens—widely applauded. One opinion survey, conducted less than a week after that fateful Tuesday, found that 89 percent of the public gave the media a positive rating. Almost a month later, approval remained high at 85 percent.

During most of the past decade, the news media seemed more national dartboard than window on the world. Coverage of the O. J. Simpson saga, the Bill Clinton–Monica Lewinsky imbroglio, the protracted 2000 presidential election, and the Chandra Levy–Gary Condit mystery both captured attention and provoked criticism. The public wondered whether journalists were reporting news or desperately trying to create it, even whether basic standards of verification and professional proportion were forgotten in a frenzy to be first or to keep a story alive.

But the calamitous events of September 11 occurred with such force and their magnitude was so profound that the news media reacted by returning to their traditional role as initial providers of previously unknown information. The story's different dimensions—the human loss, the valiant response, the national anxiety, the government's actions, the terrorists' reasons, the world's revulsion, the economic effects—deserved reporting and analysis with facts up-front. The most serious news event of the modern media age demanded the most serious journalism those media outlets could provide.

Reflecting on the response, Tom Bettag, executive producer of ABC's *Nightline*, remarks:

> I think this story is bigger than almost any breaking story we have dealt with. What made it different was the psychological shock. Journalists try to see over the horizon, to be early warning systems. The overthrow of the Shah of Iran or the taking of the hostages in Iran was not a shock. The fall of the individual states in the former Soviet empire was not a shock.
>
> Journalists are control freaks who don't like surprises. This was like the Kennedy assassination and the *Challenger* explosion. We were unprepared, shaken that we were unprepared and nearly overcome with the natural human anxiety and sadness while we were trying to do the best work of our lifetime.

Often a favorite vehicle for escape, Bettag's medium of television became a communal lifeline to the deadly reality. For the first day, a truce in competition allowed any videotape on one network to be aired by others. The round-the-clock coverage over five days after the attacks cost millions of dollars to produce—and, according to the *Wall Street Journal*, meant an estimated loss of $700 million in advertising revenues for the networks and local stations.

Television's immediacy—complete with frightfully enduring images—provided one perspective, while newspapers and other publications took another tack. Words and pictures on printed pages sought to be, in a literal sense, the first draft of history. In a remarkable return to a bygone era, more than 150 newspapers published "Extra" editions on September 11. Magazines, too, quickly followed with special issues.

Ironically, Internet websites were so bombarded with requests for instantaneous reports the day of the attacks that they couldn't handle the demand. The so-called "information superhighway" led to a dead end, only later returning to normal and to quickly constructed sources that were continually updated. Journalism itself had an inventive site discussing all facets of its work, available from the Poynter Institute for Media Studies in Saint Petersburg, Florida, at poynter.org.

Throughout the coverage, in addition to a seriousness of purpose, a new attitude pervaded the media. Gone was the snide, curled-lip cynicism of the past three decades, with its corrosive effect on what noted American philosopher William James a century ago called our "civic temper." This archly adversarial, often dismissive approach was replaced with a unifying awareness that America (its people, symbols, and ideals) was under direct attack to a degree more immediate and potentially ominous than ever before.

With the flag unavoidable on television screens and within the pages of publications, a newfound spirit of patriotism infused the media. Amid the carnage and loss of life, the valor of rescue workers and the reassurance from government officials received uplifting coverage. At the same time, almost in direct juxtaposition, the identities of the terrorists and their leaders became known, giving the enemy a human face. The inescapable fervor within communications reached the point where legitimate concern about jingoism received robust discussion.

Given the circumstances and emotions—most national journalists call New York or Washington home—newspeople struggled to find the appropriate balance between their roles as reporters and as citizens. Ever since the Vietnam War and Watergate, the media scales seemed to tip in favor of journalists hungry to investigate and expose public misdeeds and scandals. The warts and clay feet of political figures became their defining characteristics. Over time, this drumbeat of disenchantment and derision had civic consequence, producing a jaundiced view of public life that soured people's view of government, politics—and the media.

Suddenly, however, the shock of September 11 shifted the weight on the scales. Caught in the vortex of vulnerability and vicissitude, many reporters approached their work with a sense of camaraderie and purpose akin to the World War II coverage of Edward R. Murrow or Ernie Pyle. Network anchors Dan Rather and Tom Brokaw couldn't hide tears during on air interviews amid the aftermath, with Brokaw shaken when an assistant contracted anthrax handling a letter sent to him.

Shortly after September 11, when one CNN correspondent began to cry after talking with families searching for loved ones near the World Trade Center, anchor Aaron Brown broke in to console: "We are trained to be dispassionate, but we are not expected to be inhuman." The remark captured this new mood and also offered a larger lesson.

While television transmitted information and images filled with emotion, other media sought distinctive means to chronicle the events. As though traditional prose couldn't do justice to the moment, the *New Yorker, Chicago Tribune,* and other publications printed original poetry to capture and cope with the terror's tragedy. For his Saturday morning news program on National Public Radio, host Scott Simon combined reports about the aftermath with moving readings of relevant verse and the names of people either dead or missing. The *New York Times,* with coverage journalists and scholars will long study for its accomplishment and comprehensiveness, published a special section, "A Nation Challenged," each day for weeks after September 11, one page of which was always devoted to short yet poignant "Portraits of Grief" about individuals who perished.

To show the seismic shift of journalistic comportment in the wake of the attacks, editorial cartoonists put skewering caricatures aside in favor of inspiring sketches about heroism and national honor. Humor columnists, most notably Dave Barry, didn't even try to be funny, responding with sobering commentary.

Some New York–based editors and writers went so far as to suggest that irony, with its tongue-in-cheek satire and sarcastic criticism, might end altogether in this new environment of civilian carnage and high anxiety. Such pretentious (and misguided) musing was quickly disputed and rejected—the work of a Mark Twain or a Joseph Heller will always find a place in America—but it signified the extent to which some people in communication were willing to reassess the impact of mocking, even scabrous, criticism abroad in the media.

But what lasting change, if any, can the public expect in print and broadcast journalism? At this writing (in late October 2001), the media remain committed to continuing, comprehensive, and costly coverage that stresses common purpose.

As president of the Poynter Institute for Media Studies, Jim Naughton is overseeing an elaborate, multidimensional project about journalism's performance since September 11. Says Naughton, "What is happening right now is that people who consume news are getting real news, not fake news or soft features or guidance on their diet, and they are happy to have it. They're paying attention to it and valuing it."

Naughton, a veteran reporter and editor who works with college-age students as well as experienced journalists at Poynter, is particularly encouraged by the attention of one group:

> I've even begun to hope that the younger generations, the X, Y or Z people, who have been so oblivious to traditional forms of journalism, have been jostled enough by the recent events that they too are paying attention to organized media. It's been an axiom of our previous century that young Americans really did not focus on what governments and communities were doing until they settled into family relationships and had kids and worried about schools and taxes.
>
> The young generations of today have delayed way longer than their predecessors settling in to those relationships. This may be a period in which there is restoration of attention to news media by younger Americans. I would not think a smart investor would want media corporations to turn their backs on future audiences right now.

Throughout the past decade, with peace and prosperity national bywords, many communications companies closed bureaus overseas and dramatically reduced foreign coverage. In the post–Cold War world, international threats seemed remote—and bottom-line business decisions brought cheaper forms of information, what many observers dubbed "the new news," to the fore.

Now, however, the United States and journalism face a two-front war—with worry over domestic incidents, including bioterrorism, occurring at the same time the military fights abroad. Doing justice to the coverage of both fronts will require the unanticipated and long-term commitment of financial resources that will test whether news institutions remain in the business of serious news.

And, as the story continues to unfold, the media are anything but recording bystanders. All three major television networks—ABC, CBS, and NBC— were targets of anthrax attacks, a circumstance shared with several newspapers and public officials. Despite some griping that journalists were engendering fear and panic by stressing the dangers of bioterrorism, the media were dealing with the reality of specific cases and the possibility of additional ones. The emphasis served as both a national warning and potential deterrent. With the home front itself a new battlefield, the public deserves to know as much as possible.

To be sure, covering the military preparations and operations in Afghanistan and neighboring countries presents unprecedented obstacles for journalists. The shadowy, shifty nature of the enemy restricts on-the-scene reporting, resulting in reliance on government sources who (for reasons legitimate and illegitimate) often try to control what's released.

In World War II, Korea, and Vietnam, newspeople had direct access to the actions of U.S. forces. A war on terrorists (who thrive on secrecy and concealment) is decidedly different, making journalists responsible for constant evaluation of information the government makes known. Although American unity and support remain high as military involvement begins, questions cloud the future.

Will the media find reasons to correct what they're told, and, if so, how will they do it? Can the public expect an approach that's similar to the one of World War II, with its this-cause-is-noble tone, or one like Vietnam that, largely due to misleading information from public officials, found serious fault in continuing U.S. involvement? Does the shortening attention span of Americans mean the media might lose interest and shift their focus to other concerns if the war doesn't have a foreseeable ending?

Despite the new environment and its uncharted terrain, what's clear across the media is that these times still compel journalists to assume their traditional role as vigilant observers of governmental policies and actions. Criticism, even searching skepticism, will undoubtedly appear and be heard as part of the coverage.

"We'll be back to our adversarial role soon enough," comments Bettag of *Nightline*. "We weren't adversarial at the beginning of Vietnam. The Pentagon won its bet that it could get the Gulf War over before the press became adversarial. The government's role will be to reassure the public, to accent the positive. It won't be inclined to help the public grapple with tough questions.

"We're going to move into a time when hard questions will get asked about the operations in Afghanistan, about diplomatic moves and about the initial intelligence failures."

In the months ahead, journalists will have to find their balance on the new, tricky footing the war on terrorism creates. The cataclysmic events of September 11 provide a chance to reconsider attitude and behavior. Challenging, critical communication that holds the government accountable has a rightful, indeed, honored place in the American democratic system, yet— taken to extremes and to the seeming exclusion of other reportage and commentary—it imperils people's trust and risks a step back to the acidic cynicism that developed in the 1970s and prevailed through the past decade.

The first big story of the twenty-first century will set the media stage for years to come. For American journalism, what happened September 11 offers either a hopeful turning point to sustained work that fully engages reporters and citizens to meet their responsibilities or, regrettably, a missed opportunity to serve the body (and soul) politic with the more balanced approach to information purposeful self-governance requires.

—*Notre Dame Magazine*, Winter 2002

News without End

When the Television Critics Association selected *The Daily Show* on Comedy Central as the outstanding news and information program for 2004, the host of the nightly satire, Jon Stewart, acted mystified. Winner the year before for best achievement in comedy, Stewart worried the award might be a case of mistaken identity.

Outside observers had their own concerns. Were critics engaging in their own frivolity by choosing "The Most Trusted Name in Fake News" (as *The Daily Show* bills itself) over such nominees as ABC's *Nightline,* CBS's *60 Minutes,* and PBS's *Frontline?* Or has traditional journalism in America reached a crossroads, with novel forms arresting our attention and becoming influential in contemporary affairs?

A cartographer intending to map today's media world needs to work in pencil and keep a sizable eraser handy. As the communications revolution that began in the twentieth century keeps accelerating, the landscape for receiving messages seems unrecognizable from the past. New forms (via cable, satellite, and the Internet) compete with ink-on-paper publications and over-the-air broadcasts not only for a person's time but also for the way that person becomes informed.

Numbers help explain why yesterday's maps look outdated. Newspaper circulation dropped 1 percent each year from 1990 to 2002. Since 1975, across the country three hundred daily papers have gone out of business. According to a 1994 survey by the Pew Research Center for the People and the Press, 58 percent of respondents said they'd read a newspaper the day before. A decade later, the number was down to 42 percent, with those ages eighteen to twenty-nine at a mere 23 percent.

Television news, particularly at the major network level, is in sorrier shape. From peak ratings in the late 1960s, the thirty-minute nightly news broadcasts on ABC, CBS, and NBC have lost 59 percent of their collective audience. Between 1993 and 2004, Pew Center researchers found that regular watching of an evening network report declined from 60 percent of those surveyed to 34 percent.

American population is steadily increasing—203 million in 1970 to 295 million in 2005—but the consumer base of traditional news outlets is contracting. New information alternatives offer such an array of choices it's often difficult to know where to turn. In the current media world, the concept of "mass"—as in "mass audience" or "mass medium"—loses much of its prior meaning because the environment is so cluttered. Journalistic sources that didn't exist a few years ago flourish at the expense of long-established outlets.

In the same Pew Center study charting the decline in frequency for reading newspapers and watching television news, 38 percent of Americans say they regularly tune to cable news and 29 percent go to Internet news sites at least three days per week—a rise in online usage from a miniscule 2 percent in 1995. Popularity of news magazines and radio news remained fairly constant over the past decade—but neither form's current status could be confused with bygone glory days.

Then, of course, there's *The Daily Show*. What the public considers news today is vastly different from the era of "mass" outlets. Jon Stewart and his talented sidekicks focus on current subjects and journalism vulnerabilities, including network coverage, producing "fake news" that's funny and telling. Younger viewers in particular find *The Daily Show* approach engaging, ranking it highly as an influential source of what they know about contemporary affairs.

That Stewart actually interviews authentic newsmakers means that a viewer is constantly shifting back and forth between satire and some semblance of news. (John Edwards, for instance, announced his candidacy for the 2004 Democratic presidential nomination on *The Daily Show.*) The program takes delight in violating traditional journalistic canons, and in a rapidly changing information arena it wins awards.

Stewart's appropriation of news for comic purpose is by no means novel. Since the early nineteenth century, poking fun at topical targets has been a fact of American life. Mark Twain, Will Rogers, Bob Hope, and Johnny Carson all found current affairs grist for their humor mills.

What makes *The Daily Show* different is not only its bull's-eye reliance on newsy matters (momentous or momentary) but also its deliberate appearance as a television news production. The program blurs the lines dividing journalism from entertainment. What we're watching is parody, ersatz news, yet it's certainly about real news.

To a certain extent, nationally aired radio talk programs share similarities with *The Daily Show.* In high-tech symbiosis, they live off of what's being reported as news while the host provides a point of view that combines commentary and crowd-pleasing delivery. A Rush Limbaugh or an Al Franken comes across as an ideological true believer, but an impulse to amuse often animates the words. News becomes part of the personality's shtick. Is the result journalistic commentary or news-driven entertainment? Again, distinct lines aren't apparent.

What's occurring in television and radio also parallels certain practices on the Internet. Traditional news operations coexist alongside the mushrooming "blogosphere," with thousands of websites devoted to personal reactions to contemporary subjects and news coverage itself. This dual relationship expands public discourse. But does a solitary blogger, commenting on the passing scene while relying on traditional news sources, qualify as a journalist? If *The Daily Show* is fake news, is blogging really "parajournalism"—a subsidiary form inextricably linked to established institutions?

In today's tangled and thorny media world, older mainstream sources (newspapers, magazines, broadcast networks, and the like) compete with newer alternative outlets—and increasing numbers rely on the tributaries rather than the mainstream. Ready access to these new media and their messages is but one reason they're selected.

Another factor is the precipitous decline in trust and credibility experienced by traditional news organizations in recent years. Back in the 1970s, CBS news anchor Walter Cronkite led opinion surveys as "the most trusted figure" in American public life, and newspaper reporters Carl Bernstein and Bob Woodward were regarded as heroes for their investigation of Watergate. Such admiration didn't last. In the fall of 2004, a Gallup poll found just 44 percent of Americans confident of the media's ability to report news accurately and fairly.

Whether it be Jayson Blair's fabricated dispatches for the *New York Times*, the ill-sourced and irresponsible report on CBS's *60 Minutes* about President George W. Bush's National Guard service, or any of the other outrages exposed lately, flagrant unprofessionalism propels dubious citizens to other sources. The beneficiaries of mainstream media malfeasance are often the nontraditional outlets. Bloggers, in particular, can—and do—point out blatant errors, as they did with the *60 Minutes* report, and gain followers in the process.

Valuable as alternative sources might be, they pose potential problems. In most cases, serious shoe-leather reporting is secondary to commentary, and the new outlets are highly dependent on a particular point of view. Is it possible to understand different sides of an issue or problem if most of what someone knows originates at a source with a definite slant?

What we know or how we form our opinions is often the consequence of the sources to which we're exposed as contemporary affairs unfold. The Program on International Policy Attitudes at the University of Maryland released a study in autumn 2003, several months after the United States occupied Iraq, that surveyed the public's misperceptions about the war and the reasons for waging it. When questioned about three areas—evidence explicitly linking Iraq and al Qaeda, the discovery of weapons of mass destruction, and support of world opinion for American action—there was considerable disparity in people's understanding that the claims were, in fact, *not* accurate depending on the respondent's primary source of news.

According to the study, 80 percent of Fox News viewers believed one or more of the misperceptions—with those watching CBS at 71 percent, ABC at 61 percent, and both NBC and CNN at 55 percent. Readers of print sources dipped just below half at 47 percent, while followers of government-supported, commercial-free National Public Radio and the Public Broadcasting System were at the opposite end of the spectrum at 23 percent.

Of course, the Bush Administration repeated its justification for war (especially the weapons threat and the al Qaeda connection) on an almost daily basis, and those statements received consistent attention throughout the media. If over an extended period half or more of the public misunderstands matters related to war and peace, this situation in itself is reason for alarm—and criticism.

Several months after the Maryland study appeared, both the *New York Times* and the *Washington Post* published postmortems, pointing out serious lapses and problems in their preinvasion coverage. These influential newspapers, along with other outlets, kept transmitting the charge that Iraq possessed weapons of mass destruction. They did not adequately verify the veracity of the charge. Nor did they offer the views of WMD doubters, views that would have conveyed a sense of balance. Especially at a time when governmental policy makes preemptive war possible, accurate and comprehensive information is essential for public officials (and for the public at large) to evaluate the merits of taking military action.

As the news and information universe continues to expand, the discriminating citizen will need to be purposefully indiscriminate, actively selecting what's available as daily communication. One way of minimizing misunderstanding is to scrutinize several sources from varying viewpoints, encompassing traditional *and* alternative outlets.

Since the 1960s, the phrase "liberal media" has become a cliché—and for many an epithet—to describe mainstream sources. It's logical that alternative outlets would define themselves differently, distinct in approach and viewpoint. To a striking degree, these new sources challenge the "liberal media" stereotype and present themselves as an informal yet persistent check on established message makers. Realistically, however, are the premises behind such thinking valid, or is this agenda setting by another name?

Bias of some kind is inherent in human communication, but that doesn't mean every news organization thinks alike. Viewing the media as a monolith of similarly slanted messages draws into question the independent operations existing at each outlet and the competitive impulses that enliven and inspire newsrooms.

Moreover, it's difficult to figure out how seriously to take the charge of the mainstream media being liberal when you read statements of identifiable conservatives who've talked candidly about the subject. In 1992, Rich Bond, serving then as head of the Republican National Committee, confessed that claims of ideological bias weren't wholly merited. "There is some strategy to it," he told a *Washington Post* reporter. "I'm a coach of kids' basketball and Little League teams. If you watch any great coach, what they try to do is 'work the refs.' Maybe the ref will cut you a little slack on the next one."

William Kristol, a former official in Republican administrations and currently editor and publisher of the conservative magazine the *Weekly Standard*, went further when he acknowledged to the *New Yorker* in 1995: "I admit it—the liberal media were never that powerful, and the whole thing was often used as an excuse by conservatives for conservative failures." A few years later, on CNN, Kristol observed that the media weren't "as biased and liberal" as many thought. "They're actually conservative sometimes," he said.

While Bond and Kristol admit allegations of liberal bias are akin to false cries of wolf, Ari Fleischer, former presidential press secretary to George W. Bush, provides context for understanding media orientation. In his just-published memoir, *Taking Heat*, Fleischer explains: "Many Republicans, especially conservatives, believe the press are liberals who oppose Republicans and Republican ideas. I think there's an element of truth to that, but it is complicated, secondary, and often nuanced. More important, the press's first and most pressing bias is in favor of conflict and fighting. That's especially the case for the White House press corps."

As Fleischer suggests, media bias is more complicated than political or ideological preference. Structural, attitudinal, and institutional factors come into play—and carry more weight. Above all, mainstream news values a good story—one that's novel, timely, consequential, and engaging, if not compelling. The old chestnut that American journalism tries to comfort the afflicted and afflict the comfortable adds a distinct attitude—civic compassion and public accountability—to the work.

Especially when it comes to power and authority, the establishment media can be probingly skeptical. Naturally critical, these hounds of hypocrisy try to sniff out whether words match deeds and whether a figure's image conforms, as much as possible, to reality.

For those being pursued, a generalized explanation of journalistic attitude and action can mean little. In the eye of the beholder, who is also the newsmaker, the media themselves are the real problem.

Near the end of his first year as president, Bill Clinton vigorously complained to the magazine *Rolling Stone* that he didn't receive "one damn bit of credit from the knee-jerk liberal press." The two-term Democrat, so despised by conservatives, never found coverage to his liking. That he'd rail against "the knee-jerk liberal press" sounds incongruous, even ironic, but it shows the extent to which the stereotype of bias is more all-purpose accusation than demonstrable fact.

Claims of bias always depend on personal interpretation and point of view. Although those on the right tend to be more organized and vocal in their criticism, many on the left consider the establishment media as profit-obsessed operations of corporate conglomerates. In their opinion, a searching story that draws into question the larger status quo or runs the risk of alienating a sizable audience won't receive exposure for economic reasons. It's safer for the sake of the bottom line to carry an abundance of soft news and features—about celebrities, health treatments, fads, and the like.

Consistent political partiality across the mainstream media is largely mythical. If traditional journalism is so overwhelmingly slanted and influential, as some rightist critics argue, you'd think that conservative politicians would have more trouble than they do winning elections and that more than 18 percent of the public (according to a 2004 Harris poll) would identify themselves as liberal.

Be that as it may, representatives of both ends of the political spectrum agree the news reporting about certain social and cultural issues generally reflects liberal orientation. Abortion, affirmative action, gay rights, gun control, and the environment tend to receive more positive coverage, and in this sense indirectly help like-minded politicians.

Yet, serious as this situation is, other factors take precedence in explicitly political and governmental reportage. When Monica Lewinsky became a household name overnight in 1998, President Clinton's political and social views didn't make an iota of difference in the free-for-all mania to reveal sordid specifics of their relationship.

The debate over bias has become both more complicated and less meaningful in recent years. It's more complicated because the argument took root during the late 1960s, when only a few nationally significant channels of information were available. Today there are many more sources from which to choose, including some that take sides and don't aim for impartiality.

The multitude of information voices vying for attention often means a journalistic outlet takes a considered, even calculating approach to set itself apart from competitors. Some newspapers and magazines might encourage prose that features know-it-all, look-at-me "attitude," with the writer's viewpoint rivaling the subject treated. Even Associated Press, the 156-year-old wire service noted for its who-what-when-where-why reporting, recently began offering newspapers the choice of two leads for stories. While one emphasizes basic facts in straight news fashion, AP says it wants to offer the second one to "draw in the reader through imagery, narrative devices, perspective or other creative means."

On radio and television, full-throated, at times raucous, discussion frequently replaces any semblance of civil discourse. It's as though the loudest, most combative voice will stand out from the others—and thus get heard. Although such programs are carried on all-news outlets, the proximity to genuine journalism is remote. Part personal prejudice, part ego gratification, heat rather than light usually results.

With the media multiplying like kudzu and the mainstream shrinking, there might seem less at stake in the controversy over bias. In an era of deep political divisions, however, messengers carrying political messages are as vulnerable to criticism as partisan politicians. Indeed, the media-bias debate feeds political polarization in the United States by making the public suspicious of what they read, see, and hear from the left, right, and center.

Consider the titles of recent books about the media, several of which became national bestsellers: *Bias: A CBS Insider Exposes How the Media Distort the News* by Bernard Goldberg; *Slander: Liberal Lies about the American Right* by Ann Coulter; *What Liberal Media? The Truth about BIAS and the News* by Eric Alterman; *Lies (and the Lying Liars Who Tell Them): A Fair and Balanced Look at the Right* by Al Franken; *Big Lies: The Right-Wing Propaganda Machine and How It Distorts the Truth* by Joe Conason; and *Weapons of Mass Distortion: The Coming Meltdown of the Liberal Media* by L. Brent Bozell III.

With all the allegations about lying, bias, and distortion, it's difficult to see how anything resembling truth could ever emerge. One person's polluted channel for information is another's invaluable source—and the debate is frequently far from polite. In *Slander*, Coulter remarks: "Journalism is war by other means." That seems a restrictive definition, but the intellectual issue isn't exactly joined when Franken in his book dismisses Coulter as a "nutcase." Rather than trying to provoke thought, these books provide poison-tipped ammunition for like-minded believers. That they sell so well speaks volumes about entrenched, ideological opinions and fervor, daily stoked, that won't easily fade.

Although the media-bias debate (in books, articles, talk shows, and elsewhere) often appears as a sideshow to the center-ring argument between conservatives and liberals over the nation's direction and political issues, it's taking place as the public tries to figure out how best to navigate through all the available news and information.

In this new milieu, the mainstream media no longer exert the hold they once did. Other voices are being heard, and some of those voices critique media performance and perceived slanting for whatever motivation.

Fox News Channel might promote "fair and balanced" news coverage, but that slogan is about as truthful and self-serving as the one published on every edition of the *New York Times*: "All the News That's Fit to Print." Fox News found its niche by defining its messages differently from others in TV journalism. Begun in 1996 and inspired in part by the success of talk radio, the channel wasn't afraid to be perceived as having a point of view. That style attracted viewers, propelling Fox News into the lead of cable news organizations. Significantly, during the 2004 Republican National Convention, Fox News had a larger audience than any of the three broadcast networks (ABC, CBS, NBC) and over three times the viewership of either MSNBC or CNN. By taking a point of view, the channel is building a following that's worth watching on its own.

To what extent does the success of Fox signal a return to a partisan press in America? In the nation's early years, newspapers made no effort to be neutral, a practice that continues in Britain, Europe, and elsewhere. If the news audience expects a particular slant, charges of bias become meaningless. This, however, comes at the expense of not learning certain aspects of a story or never hearing a contrary opinion about a subject.

With ideologically oriented information, the content has a predictability that puts it in the category of preaching to an already assembled and faithful choir. What's reported might introduce new information, but the larger objective involves reinforcing someone's viewpoint and opinions. The approach also tends to deepen political and social divisions—and to stifle more comprehensive inquiry. Instead of fostering fuller understanding, sides are taken, fingers are pointed, and blame is assessed.

What complicates any discussion of today's media environment in the United States is the variety of different messages circulating at a given time. A newspaper, for example, might try to present its reportage with (in Irish writer and statesman Edmund Burke's phrase) "the cold neutrality of an impartial judge," but commentary columns and editorials frequently make readers think they detect a distinct perspective. In news magazines and on broadcast media, analysis and interpretation often seem to mingle with personal opinion. Trying to keep types of journalism and different sources straight becomes difficult for the public.

Most media don't take enough care to explain their work or to make the necessary distinctions among different journalistic forms. How many faithfully follow the famous dictum "fact is sacred, opinion is free"? Compounding the problem are the new, alternative sources of information that rely on the news for their content but follow their own agendas and prejudices. In this increasingly crowded and noisy arena, distinguishing between journalism and entertainment or journalism and "parajournalism" can be difficult. There are no bright, bold lines marking off balanced, complete reporting (of the just-the-facts school) from selective, slanted opinion offerings.

To be sure, a citizen's access to a wide range of fact and opinion has never been greater. For example, through cable outlets (including C-SPAN) and Internet sites, it's now relatively easy to watch or read the entirety of speeches, news conferences, and other presentations, allowing someone to evaluate and judge a source without outside interference.

But that admirably independent approach now openly competes with its opposite: point-of-view reporting and analysis that originates with an agenda or purpose. These sources can be valuable—bloggers, say, can keep a story alive by investigating it from other angles and by pushing the traditional media to correct an original account—but the trick is to avoid what media theorists call "information segregation."

When this happens, people rely on outlets with which they already agree. They don't seek contrasting information. This method of media selection— and personal bias—results in the possibility of never understanding an issue as completely as possible or even very well.

Different technologies now make it possible to receive personally designed, tailor-made collections of reportage, analysis, and commentary that observers have dubbed "The Daily Me." But if the "Me" too narrowly defines the information provided—a preponderance of entertainment or sports news, political information from one perspective, economic or business reports but little else—there's the danger of not receiving a thorough, reliable picture of America or the world.

The Daily Show and "The Daily Me" challenge conventional thinking about news, but they symbolize our times and future—with definitions changing, traditions ending, lines blurring. With the media world teeming with choice, our relationship to it will be radically different, as we try to deal with the endless welter of messages. "Keeping up" with contemporary affairs (a civic notion of an earlier era with far fewer sources) will demand a conscious effort of constant scrutiny. The age-old worry over gaining access to information is over. Now it's a matter of selection and attention—and assuming new obligations of twenty-first-century citizenship.

—Notre Dame Magazine, Summer 2005

HEADNOTE

My interest in Ben Hecht began by chance. A letter from the editor of a volume in the series *Dictionary of Literary Biography* offered potential contributors a list of American short-story writers he wanted to include. From growing up near Chicago and indiscriminately reading the city's newspapers, I knew Hecht's name and his association with the frequently mentioned play *The Front Page*, which defined the hell-bent-for-story approach of Chicago journalism that took root early in the twentieth century.

Since the contributed article appeared in 1989—in preparing it I discovered that Hecht published approximately 250 short stories—I have written several essays, both academic and popular, about Hecht and his work. The sheer volume of what he wrote and the utterly engaging yet utterly unreliable explanations of his output and life establish barriers to biographical studies and comprehensive analytical assessments. In addition, legal strictures prohibiting direct quoting from unpublished manuscripts (many about Chicago) make a complete survey of the kind I'd like to do impossible at this time. Hecht, however, was an authentic American original, never failing to provide the delight of discovery.

Ben Hecht and Chicago

Studying Ben Hecht's papers at Chicago's Newberry Library for a prospective book is less an academic exercise than a mental game akin to assembling a complicated jigsaw puzzle. Box upon box (sixty-seven in all) reveals an imaginative and prolific author whose literary productivity defies easy classification or assessment. Trying to figure out how all the pieces of his creativity fit together becomes the trick.

In more than a half century of writing, Hecht completed ten novels, approximately 250 short stories, some twenty plays, scores of screenplays, numerous radio and TV scripts, four memoirs, two collections of newspaper columns (selected from a prodigious output of journalism), two books about Jewish affairs, and more than the occasional poem. In addition, neatly stored in those boxes at the Newberry are quite a few unfinished or unpublished efforts.

Yet for Hecht, who died at age seventy in 1964, statistics tell just a fraction of the story. As a Chicago journalist from 1910 to 1924, he was known as a star reporter and popular columnist—so popular that his still-engrossing collection of sketches, *1001 Afternoons in Chicago*, was proclaimed a classic and "something of a Bible" for newspaper writers nationally after it appeared eighty years ago this year.

At the same time, Hecht turned out avant-garde fiction, poetry, and drama that earned him a place (alongside Sherwood Anderson, Carl Sandburg, Maxwell Bodenheim, and others) in the Chicago literary renaissance.·

His original story for the 1927 movie *Underworld* won the first Academy Award for writing given by Hollywood. In 1928, *The Front Page*, a play coauthored with Charles MacArthur, became a Broadway triumph and (in the phrase of Tennessee Williams years later) "took the corsets off the American theater."

Hecht's youthful genre-hopping, combined with rapid completion of projects, set patterns for his work that continued throughout his life. Joseph Epstein, who teaches literature and writing at Northwestern University, shrewdly appraised Hecht's career by calling him "the great hack genius."

The paradox of Epstein's phrase—how many hacks are geniuses?—points out a central problem in evaluating Hecht. Throw in the definite article "the" along with the adjective "great" and you, of course, compound the problem.

Hecht himself realized the difficulty presented anyone trying to survey what he did. At the beginning of his 654-page autobiography, *A Child of the Century* (1954), he says: "I can understand the literary critic's shyness toward me. It is difficult to praise a novelist or a thinker who keeps popping up as the author of innumerable movie melodramas. It is like writing about the virtues of a preacher who keeps carelessly getting himself arrested in bordellos."

From his early days in Chicago through the nearly four decades he divided his time between New York and Hollywood, Hecht approached what he wrote from distinct perspectives. Some projects (such as the 1939 novella collection *A Book of Miracles* and *A Child of the Century*) he considered serious literary works. Others were mercenary ventures to subsidize the writing he cared about, causes he adopted (most notably, saving European Jews from the Holocaust), and a comfortable, bicoastal standard of living.

Though he rarely missed a chance to belittle the assembly-line process of screenwriting, many clipped-and-saved gossip columns in the Newberry report $1,000-per-day or $10,000-per-week assignments in Hollywood to deliver or doctor a script. Some films Hecht worked on include *The Scoundrel* (which won him another Oscar), *Stagecoach*, *Gone with the Wind*, *Spellbound*, *Notorious*—even *Queen of Outer Space* and *The 7 Faces of Dr. Lao*.

French director Jean-Luc Godard said in the late 1960s that Hecht "invented 80 percent of what is used in American movies today." The creator of cinematic stereotypes wasn't shy about using those stereotypes and others to dash off a screenplay, story treatment, or scene change. Frequently, as with *Gone with the Wind* and several of Alfred Hitchcock's most celebrated films, the work was lucrative yet went uncredited on the screen.

Common to all of Hecht's writing is a vivid, energetic style, with charged phrasing that crackles and explodes with immediacy and force. He emphasizes stories that are telling and well told, to the extent that *A Child of the Century*, which he calls "an autobiography of my mind," is really an extended collection of personal tales. Their veracity is at times suspect—Norman Mailer once said, "Hecht was never a writer to tell the truth when a concoction could put life in his prose"—but the inventive rendering carries the narrative (and the reader) along.

The sheer volume of writing Hecht left behind certainly suggests a speed in composition most wordsmiths, serious or otherwise, would envy. Although trained as a reporter to turn out copy on a typewriter, his papers show he quickly shifted to pencil and cheap, unlined sheets—which often reflect minimal revision when compared to the final version.

Wearing down what he estimated to an interviewer were "75 to 100 pencils a week," Hecht never seemed at a loss for words. His apprenticeship in journalism might have taught him he didn't want to keep pounding a typewriter (he preferred sitting in a comfortable chair and scribbling on a writing board), but it instilled in him the done-in-a-day conditioning reporters learn for completing assignments under strict deadlines.

Hecht's Chicago years also proved significant in selecting subjects he wrote about after he departed for New York and Hollywood. His novel *Count Bruga*, published in 1926, comically portrays poet Hippolyt Bruga, a not-overly-fictionalized depiction of Bodenheim. Stories for the films *Underworld* and *Scarface* draw on a reporter's memory of gangster comportment and crime in the city. *The Front Page*, considered by most theater critics one of the finest American stage comedies (and the inspiration for four movies, including *His Girl Friday*), brings to life competitive shenanigans of Chicago journalists while poking fun at local politics and police activity.

Although he ridiculed Chicago and asserted its "reputation as a cultural center is a myth" in what seemed to be a good-riddance essay for the *New Yorker* in 1925, his outlook dramatically changed shortly thereafter. In the epilogue to the published version of *The Front Page*, which went through several printings, Hecht and MacArthur (a former *Chicago Tribune* reporter) offer an "apology" for initially setting out to criticize journalism and Chicago:

It developed in writing this play that our contempt for the institution of the Press was a bogus attitude; that we looked back on the Local Room where we had spent half our lives as a veritable fairyland—and that we were both full of nostalgia for the bouncing days of our servitude.

The same uncontrollable sentimentality operated in our treatment of Chicago which, as much as any of our characters, is the hero of our play.

The iniquities, double dealings, chicaneries and immoralities which as ex-Chicagoans we knew so well returned to us in a mist called the Good Old Days, and our delight in our memories would not be denied.

For Hecht, the "Good Old Days" of his Chicago youth strikingly return with robust, albeit often romanticized, intensity during his last decade in four books. More than one-third of *A Child of the Century* concerns his time as a reporter and first steps as a serious writer. He produced the biography-memoir *Charlie* in 1957, the year after MacArthur died, with the most vibrant sections about his frequent collaborator's life during their joint time in Chicago.

Seven years later, *Gaily, Gaily* appeared, focusing directly on roistering high jinks and ribald antics of Hecht's first five years as a young reporter, beginning in 1910 at sixteen. A year later, not long after he died, *Letters from Bohemia* came out. The publisher termed the writer's final book a "nostalgic memoir," with Chicago reminiscences about (among others) Anderson, Bodenheim, and MacArthur included.

In curious literary symmetry, Hecht spent much of his last decade reliving in his imagination and through words his first decade as a reporter and aspiring author. Besides the four autobiographical books from 1954 to 1964, he also published several magazine articles and turned out scripts referring back to his youthful years.

"I find an increasing tendency when writing of myself to tell pleasant lies," Hecht once said. This impulse to fabricate (did he really, for instance, produce a mystery novel, *The Florentine Dagger*, in thirty-six hours to win a bet?) complicates anyone's understanding of the writer, especially what he says in his late-life memoirs. That he repeats certain stories, changing and embellishing circumstances and details, makes matters even more difficult.

Interestingly, right up to the day he died, Hecht kept working on what he hoped would be a grand Broadway production about the rivalry between Italian and Irish mobs in Chicago during Prohibition. Drafts of the never-produced musical (which began as a play) are among Hecht's papers and propose several possible titles: "Chicago," "Chicago Days," "Chicago Nights," "Underworld," and "Angel in the Underworld."

Ernest Hemingway called the Paris of his early years "a moveable feast." For Hecht, Chicago was that—and much more. Here, however, speculation intrudes on sources, leading to questions about his preoccupation with a specific city at a particular time. Was it an aging author's nostalgia for years of initiation and discovery? Was it the rosy recollection of a period of intently lived experience before becoming something of a perpetual-motion writing machine? Was it the celebration of a time of literary promise that seemed artistically idyllic—and in contrast to his Hollywood hackery? Was it a way of trying to escape the horrors of the Holocaust that haunted so much of his thinking throughout the 1940s? Was it the combination of several motivations Hecht himself couldn't articulate?

Occasionally, in the memoirs, clues appear. In A *Child of the Century*, for example, he writes:

> My years in Chicago were a bright time spent in the glow of new worlds. I was a newspaper reporter, playwright, novelist, short-story writer, propagandist, publisher and crony of wild hearts and fabulous gullets. I haunted streets, studios, whore houses, police stations, courtrooms, theater stages, jails, saloons, slums, mad houses, fires, murders, riots, banquet halls and bookshops. I ran everywhere in the city like a fly buzzing in the works of a clock, tasted more than any fly belly could hold, learned not to sleep (an accomplishment that still clings to me) and buried myself in a tick-tock of whirling hours that still echo in me.

A few pages later, he explains himself in relation to Chicago: "I have lived in other cities but been inside only one. I knew Chicago's thirty-two feet of intestines. Only newspapermen ever achieve this bug-in-a-rug citizenship."

Recalling his past and moving to New York in *Charlie*, Hecht goes so far as to confess: "We were all fools to have left Chicago. It was a town to play in;

a town where you could stay yourself, and where the hoots of the critics couldn't frighten your style or drain your soul."

A more telling rationale for Hecht's obsession with Chicago comes from someone who knew him well from the late 1920s on, actress Helen Hayes. Widow of MacArthur and longtime New York neighbor, she spoke about "Ben and Charlie" at a Newberry Library dinner in 1980 after the arrival of Hecht's papers there.

"Ben was never comfortable in the adult world," Hayes said. "He spent his whole life trying to hang on to youth, its mindset, its wonderment, its carefree fizz."

Most of Ben Hecht's enduring work—for the theater, on the movie screen, and in prose—uses his youthful Chicago days for inspiration. This child of the twentieth century always carried the City of the Big Shoulders around in his imagination, producing words that still reverberate today.

Reading Ben Hecht

Here are twelve works by Ben Hecht that show his breadth as a writer and help explain his life:

Erik Dorn (1921). A novel, featuring a Chicago reporter involved in a love triangle, that captures post–World War I disillusionment and urban angst with lacerating epigrams and brooding digressions.

1001 Afternoons in Chicago (1922). Memorable newspaper sketches that reveal the city and its people with sensitivity and panache.

Broken Necks (1926). Short stories that reflect small-magazine literary experimentation and savvy understanding of mass-market fiction.

The Front Page (1928). An enduring portrait of wisecracking, scoop-minded reporters that helped define the Chicago school of news and the broader public's view of journalism.

A Book of Miracles (1939). Seven artfully crafted novellas that explore spiritual concerns through distinctive characters and ingenious plots.

1001 Afternoons in New York (1941). Sharp-edged newspaper columns that evoke pre–World War II America and make a case for the urgent need to help European Jews escape Nazi persecution.

A Guide for the Bedevilled (1944). An extended personal and passionate essay on the evils of anti-Semitism, by a writer previously unconcerned about his own Jewishness.

The Collected Stories of Ben Hecht (1945). A compendium of short fiction by an inventive storyteller who takes on a variety of subjects and narrative techniques.

A Child of the Century (1954). A sprawling autobiography that not only dramatizes the author's life but also allows him to speak his mind on long-nursed grudges and abiding obsessions.

Charlie: The Improbable Life and Times of Charles MacArthur (1957). An anecdote-filled portrait of the former Chicago reporter, who went on to write Broadway plays and Hollywood movies, often in collaboration with Hecht.

Perfidy (1961). Controversial and polemical account of the establishment of Israel and the Jewish state's early leadership.

Gaily, Gaily (1963). Adult adventures of a callow Chicago reporter that mingle memory and imagination to produce cleverly rendered tales of initiation and self-discovery.

—*Chicago Tribune*, March 31, 2002

The Front Page Turns Seventy-Five

"The son of a bitch stole my watch!"

With the brio of a bold but beautiful lie, the curtain falls to conclude the last act of *The Front Page*.

Managing editor Walter Burns is hell-bent to see his ace reporter, Hildy Johnson, stay in journalism, so he concocts a criminal charge to bring Hildy back to Chicago. Immediately, the audience realizes the ruse of a trumped-up theft will return the reporter to the city—and newspaper—that in his ink-stained heart of hearts, he doesn't want to leave. The duo's adventures of bedeviling politicians, revealing love nests, and selling newspapers will continue, edition after edition.

The Front Page is the play that never ends.

For seventy-five years, since its sensational Broadway opening on August 14, 1928, stage and screen productions of *The Front Page* have dramatized journalistic behavior—and misbehavior—as the life of an accused (albeit pathetic) killer hangs in the balance. Corrupt, vote-hungry public officials, psychotic policemen, a heart-of-gold streetwalker, and Hildy's long-suffering fiancée season the action, but newspeople occupy center stage.

The Front Page has been called the Rosetta stone of journalism, the key to figuring out the hieroglyphics and high jinks of a strange craft. It's also in many ways a theatrical Rorschach test. While most journalists and kindred spirits applaud the anarchic antics and comic cynicism involved in covering a big story, others find the ostentatious irresponsibility and unswerving devotion to sensationalism an amusing affirmation of their complaints about the press. To love or to loathe—that is the question.

Though simple in structure and staging—every moment of the three acts takes place during a single evening in the Press Room of Chicago's Criminal Courts Building—the portrayal of journalists pursuing a life-or-death story is arrestingly (and deceptively) complex. Burns and Johnson save a condemned man from the gallows, but amid the hilarity questions arise.

Is this really how news gets made? Does competition drive coverage to the exclusion of scruples? How seriously should anyone take the final product of work so laughably rendered?

Although Walter Burns seems incapable of personal or professional doubt—most of his utterances, the audience understands, are deliberately untruthful (and, hence, more entertaining)—Hildy Johnson harbors reservations. Strolling into the play intending to leave his newspaper job to get married and join a New York advertising firm, he lectures his Press Room sidekicks: "Journalists! Peeking through keyholes! Running after fire engines like a lot of coach dogs! Waking people up in the middle of the night to ask them what they think of Mussolini. Stealing pictures off old ladies of their daughters that get raped in Oak Park. A lot of lousy, daffy buttinskis, swelling around with holes in their pants, borrowing nickels from office boys! And for what? So a million hired girls and motormen's wives'll know what's going on."

When another reporter accuses Johnson of discoursing under the influence of blinding love, Hildy fires back: "I don't need anybody to tell me about newspapers. I've been a newspaperman fifteen years. A cross between a bootlegger and a whore."

Hildy's fulminations are funny—and typical of the top-of-the-lung dialogue throughout *The Front Page*. They also help establish the play's dramatic tension. Try as he might to free himself from his all-consuming work for the romance of marital, ad-agency bliss, the competing seduction of journalism keeps luring him back. It's a business he both hates *and* loves, with the ambivalence animating all three acts.

In his theater critic days at the *New York Times*, Frank Rich referred to *The Front Page* as "one play that will never receive a negative review in a newspaper." Cheering from the press seats began with the première seventy-five years ago.

"Until the production of *The Front Page* no good newspaper play had ever been written in this country," noted Heywood Broun in his first-night review for the *New York Telegram*. "And that is curious, for there is no other field in which one may find so many engaging persons, all of them completely mad. There is slight rational basis on which a man may say: 'I'll die for the dear old *Bugle*.' And yet he would."

Broun, who later remarks that those "addicted to cocaine or newspaper work never do get cured entirely," captures the maddening magnetism of journalism the play brings to life. Other opening-night reviewers identified different qualities.

In the *New York World*, Alison Smith effused, ". . . *The Front Page* with its rowdy virility, its swift percussion of incident, its streaks of Gargantuan derision, is as breath-taking an event as ever dropped, with or without warning, into the middle of a becalmed August on Broadway. . . . It is almost unbelievably exciting when, as at this opening, it recaptures the mockery, the disillusion and the fierce unreasoning loyalty of that dusty, clattering, smoke-filled world with the grimy label of 'Press' above its door."

Although much of the play's force and authenticity comes from its life-like language—Hildy calls Burns a "paranoiac bastard," "lousy baboon," and "double-crossing louse," while Walter's all-purpose expletive is "H. Sebastian God!"—reviewers shied away from direct quotation. In the *Herald Tribune*, Percy Hammond informs readers that the script is "a complete glossary of profanity, useful to those who wish to learn the art." He renders the last line with dashes, "The — — — stole my watch!" and concludes his paean: "There are more meaty wise cracks by reporters in ten minutes of *The Front Page* than I have heard in seven years' association with *Herald Tribune* men; and I hope the boys will see the play and learn to be more amusing."

How the *New York Times*—which one of the Chicago reporters in the play quit because "You might as well work in a bank"—handled the new Broadway hit became a mini-drama in itself. Lead reviewer J. Brooks Atkinson extolled the "loud, rapid, coarse and unfailing entertainment" of "a racy story with all the tang of front page journalism" in his immediate response for next-morning readers.

Oddly, his judgment of the dialogue tries to have it both ways. "In the escape of a prisoner just on the eve of a political execution, and in the draggle-tailed characters involved, the authors have such a picturesque yarn to spin that their insistence upon thrusting bespattered conversation down the throats of the audience is as superfluous as it is unpleasant." That sentence, though, is followed with this one: "No one who has ground his heels in the grime of a police headquarters press room will complain that this argot misrepresents the gentlemen of the press."

But eleven days later in a centerpiece essay for the Sunday drama and music section, Atkinson argues that the play's language "bruises the sensitive ear with a Rabelaisian vernacular unprecedented for its up-hill and downdale blasphemy." Calling the "grossness of the dialogue distasteful," he offers a different opinion from his initial one on the verisimilitude of the reporters' lingo: ". . . *The Front Page* smites the ears roundly with the argot of the gutter. Quite apart from its authenticity, which may be disputed, it adds a fresh peril to casual playgoing for purposes of entertainment."

Why the change of opinion and high-decibel criticism? Did Atkinson have second thoughts of his own, or were they suggested to him? What's known is that Adolph Ochs, the publisher of the *Times*, hated the portrayal of the press in *The Front Page* and sought to have it suppressed. Unsuccessful at that, he had the paper's attorney, George Gordon Battle, write a lengthy signed editorial, "Stage Profanity Again Under Fire," which appeared two Sundays after Atkinson's revisionist assault. Observing that the "unprecedented vulgarity" of the dialogue make it "entirely impossible to reproduce in the columns of a newspaper designed for general circulation the language used in this play," Battle has a more substantive complaint—and worry.

What he solemnly calls "the newspaper profession" stood in jeopardy of losing public esteem: "If these attacks upon the press in the guise of dramatic representation are allowed to continue unanswered, and even approved, by the representatives of the press, inevitably the public will believe them to be true. The result will be increased distrust in the truthfulness and reliability of the press in general."

The Ochs-Battle effort to kill interest in *The Front Page* failed. Even before Battle's editorial appeared, the play's producer, Jed Harris, was featured on the cover of *Time*, trumpeting the "new season's first hit . . . full of sound and flurry." Success on Broadway—276 performances at a time when 100 shows were considered respectable—quickly resulted in productions elsewhere, including Chicago and Los Angeles.

Ironically, one *Times* staffer took particular delight in the laughter coming from Times Square Theatre during the play's initial run of eight months. Playwright and wit George S. Kaufman also served as the paper's drama editor throughout the 1920s. Harris asked Kaufman to try his hand at directing, with *The Front Page* Kaufman's first of many triumphs. If Ochs and Battle were worried about "the newspaper profession" and how it was perceived, their concern (it would seem) didn't extend to potential conflicts of interest.

Kaufman's involvement in *The Front Page* was critical to its success. When fledgling dramatists Ben Hecht and Charles MacArthur approached Harris with the draft of a play that drew on their experiences as Chicago reporters circa 1920, the producer saw many possibilities and several problems.

According to Harris in his memoir, *A Dance on the High Wire*, he angered Hecht and MacArthur when he told them: "We are going to have a really great show. All we have to do is throw out the second and third acts and start from the end of the first act —"

Despite threats to take their play to another producer, Harris explained the need for "a single line of action" to hold the scenes together, even proposing "some crooked device" to end act 3 and the play—as it turned out the putatively purloined watch. The theme, in his bold formulation, was "once you get caught in the lousy newspaper business you can never get out again."

How extensively Kaufman personally revised the original script is unknown, but Broadway historians trace the fast pace and overlapping dialogue to Kaufman and techniques he used in earlier comedies he'd written, including *The Cocoanuts* for the Marx Brothers. Harris even credits the novice director with coming up with the play's title, a matter of continuing dispute.

As might be expected, neither Hecht nor MacArthur conceded any authorship to Kaufman for *The Front Page*. Although Hecht wrote engagingly about his roistering days as a reporter and young author in four separate books, including *A Child of the Century* (1954) and *Gaily, Gaily* (1963), a lack of consistency in remembering and a love for embellishing his past to tell more engaging stories make him a dubious source.

With that caveat, in his 1957 book about his recently deceased collaborator and friend, *Charlie: The Improbable Life and Times of Charles MacArthur*, Hecht explains the writing process that produced their best-known play and several other popular works for stage and screen: "I sat with a pencil, paper and a lap board. Charlie walked, lay on a couch, looked out of a window, drew mustaches on magazine cover girls, and prowled around in some fourth dimension. Out of him, during these activities, came popping dialogue and plot turns. A single quality was in them. They were always true. It was always a character who spoke, not a line born of another line."

Seven years later, however, in the posthumously published volume *Letters from Bohemia*, Hecht's recollection changes: "I wrote more of the dialogue and came up with more of the plot turns, but it was Charlie who was more the playwright. He loved the stage more."

This version has corroboration. Actress Helen Hayes, who married MacArthur shortly after *The Front Page* opened, told the *New York Times* in 1986 that Hecht was responsible for "most of the dialogue" and "the plot turns." In the interview, timed to coincide with one of the play's many New York revivals, she said: "Charlie created the characters. He knew those fellows inside and out, he knew their souls."

In particular MacArthur knew the soul of Walter Burns. He based the character on his former editor at the *Chicago Examiner*, Walter Howey, one of William Randolph Hearst's more colorful and hard-charging employees. According to MacArthur, Howey kept resignations of several public officials in his desk and threatened to use them if anything they did upset the power-savvy, manipulating editor. To believe reminiscences about Howey by both MacArthur and Hecht their Burns, always aflame with schemes of scoops, displays less unscrupulous ingenuity than his real-life model.

Yet the Burns we see in action—and much of the play's sense of action comes from the rapid-fire dialogue and the quick thinking behind it—is an editor and person to behold. His damn-the-competition single-mindedness is funny—at one point he admits to Hildy he "was in love once—with my third wife"—but more serious on reflection.

Just as the fun-loving, boys-will-be-boys reporters end up getting rough with "North Clark Street tart" Mollie Malloy in a scene that leads her to jump out a window, a brass-knuckled reality keeps intruding on the comedy, giving it unexpected depth and dimension. When the mayor and sheriff threaten Walter and Hildy with arrest for hiding "a fugitive from justice," Burns reminds the authorities of people who died trying to take on the *Examiner.*

The play's first Broadway run set the stage for what turned out to be a multimedia future. A New York publisher rushed a hardback reader's edition to bookstores across the country. Its popularity (three printings the first three months, with three more the first year) made what the authors advertised in the publisher's catalogue as "a great work of art, something like Hamlet" the first theatrical script to sell well as a book in America.

Included in the reader's version, often anthologized in collections of America's greatest plays, were not only the characters' memorable lines but also additional background and commentary, principally disguised as directions. Hecht and MacArthur wanted their say, too, with neither shy about offering an opinion.

Before Hildy utters a word, we learn: "Hildy is of a vanishing type—the lusty, hoodlumesque half-drunken caballero that was the newspaperman of our youth. Schools of journalism and the advertising business have nearly extirpated the species. Now and then one of these boys still pops up in the profession and is hailed by his editor as a survival of a golden age. . . . Their presence under one roof [in the play's Press Room] is due to the fact that Chicago is a sort of journalistic Yellowstone Park offering haven to a last herd of fantastic bravos that once roamed the newspaper offices of the country."

When Walter Burns enters near the end of act 2, the description is less warmly nostalgic and more darkly satiric: "Beneath a dapper and very citizen-like exterior lurks a hobgoblin, perhaps the devil himself. . . . In less hyperbolic language, Mr. Burns is that product of thoughtless, pointless, nerve-drumming unmorality that is the Boss Journalist—the licensed eavesdropper, trouble maker, bombinator and Town Snitch, misnamed the Press."

Hecht and MacArthur used the added text to round out what the characters represented and why they acted (and talked) as they did. Unlike the performance script with its just-the-facts directions—"Walter Burns enters. Stands up Center."—the authors had some fun of their own, usually at the expense of journalism.

Most significantly, Hecht and MacArthur appended an epilogue after the memorable last line that puts the previous 189 pages in perspective. In effect, they confess, we didn't mean it. Despite the criticism and sarcasm directed at the news business, the authors pine for bygone days of scoring scoops and deflating windbags:

When we applied ourselves to write a newspaper play we had in mind a piece of work which would reflect our intellectual disdain of and superiority to the Newspaper.

What we finally turned out, as the reader may verify if he will, is a romantic and rather doting tale of our old friends—the reporters of Chicago.

It developed in writing this play that our contempt for the institution of the Press was a bogus attitude; that we looked back on the Local Room where we had spent half our lives as a veritable fairyland—and that we were both full of a nostalgia for the bouncing days of our servitude.

By combining what they call "oaths and realisms" about journalism with unfolding action that dramatizes an editor and reporter's obsessive drive for a good story, Hecht and MacArthur create "a Valentine thrown to the past"— but one that arrives with a bill of particulars as the inscription.

These self-described "reporters in exile" do more than retreat to their joint youth for a period piece of passing diversion. They establish a portrayal of the press with timeless relevance, their Rosetta stone also serving as a springboard.

With its vivid characters and fast-paced wisecracking, *The Front Page* was a natural for Hollywood and its new innovation, "talking pictures." The first of four major-studio adaptations of the play came out in 1931, featuring Pat O'Brien as Hildy and Adolphe Menjou as Walter. Nominated for three Academy Awards, including best picture, the film's popularity helped spark production over the next decade of several other movies focusing on newspaper life.

Some—notably *Front Page Woman* (1935) and *The Girl on the Front Page* (1936)—sought direct association with the original play and film. Others emphasized the hurly-burly of journalism in their titles: *The Final Edition* (1932), *Headline Shooters* (1934), *Exclusive Story* (1936), and *Exclusive* (1937). In 1937, Hecht, a prolific and highly paid scriptwriter, composed the screenplay for *Nothing Sacred*, giving him another chance to mock the mores of the press. As one character growls: "I'll tell you briefly what I think of newspapermen. The hand of God reaching down into the mire couldn't elevate one of them to the depths of degradation. Not by a million miles."

Ultimately, the flurry of films about the Fourth Estate produced Orson Welles's fictionalized and controversial portrait of Hearst, *Citizen Kane*, released in 1941. The year before, though, noted director Howard Hawks took *The Front Page* and transformed it into *His Girl Friday*.

Retaining the basic storyline of ace reporter and devilishly creative editor trying to beat the competition by hiding an escaped criminal, Hawks made Hildy a woman (Rosalind Russell), who was recently divorced from Walter (Cary Grant). Hildy plans to remarry and leave journalism—but, of course, the big story intervenes.

Considered one of the funniest, most sophisticated screwball comedies of that Depression-era genre, *His Girl Friday* strengthens the original play's theme—once a journalist always a journalist—while adding sexual electricity between the two main characters. Double entendres replace profane outbursts, and the new Hildy is just as competitive and ballsy as any male Hildebrand Johnson.

In *Hawks on Hawks*, the director explains the celluloid sex change. Recalling that he told a dinner party "the finest modern dialogue in the world came from Hecht and MacArthur," he took two copies of *The Front Page* and had a woman read Hildy's lines, while he spoke Walter's. Hawks found the exchange more lively and promising.

"See, *The Front Page* was intended as a love affair between two men," Hawks declared. "I mean, they *loved* each other. There's no doubt about it."

In either rendering, however, the true journalist's love of a breaking story is really more indomitable than interpersonal association of whatever kind. Hildy and Walter hear different voices of the same calling. How they respond to those individual voices keeps them together.

Even with the success of *His Girl Friday*, Hollywood wasn't finished with *The Front Page*—or *His Girl Friday*. In 1974, Billy Wilder, a reporter in Vienna and Berlin before emigrating to America to make films, paired Walter Matthau and Jack Lemmon as Burns and Johnson in a scenically stylish remake of the original play.

What's missing, though, is the substantively acute treatment of journalism that Wilder brought to his 1951 film *Ace in the Hole* (also known as *The Big Carnival*). Matthau and Lemmon seem to play themselves from earlier comic movies rather than the more complicated characters created by Hecht and MacArthur. The "real" Walter Burns relishes the influence he can wield over others and an entire city. Matthau as Burns is more intent on portraying an irascible curmudgeon.

The mediocre reviews Wilder's rendition received didn't stop Hollywood from committing yet another remake. In 1988, *Switching Channels* attempted to update *His Girl Friday*. Kathleen Turner was the reporter (renamed Christy Colleran) and Burt Reynolds her news executive ex-husband (called, remarkably, John L. Sullivan IV). The different names are the first of many indecent liberties taken with *The Front Page/His Girl Friday*. In this production, Christy plays a television reporter for the Satellite News Network, based in Chicago. Instead of a rolltop desk, the escaped prisoner hides in a copying machine. Critics knowledgeable of the film's ancestry howled.

The various film versions still often appear on television, sometimes with two or three airing consecutively, showing the story's protean adaptability. The small screen also made its own use of the original play. Back in 1949 and 1950, CBS created an entire series based on and called *The Front Page*. Although lasting several months, segments lacked the compressed energy, snappy dialogue, and single-story mania of the series' namesake. Interestingly, *TV Guide* found another reason to dislike the series: "We have come to know that newspapermen are literate, well-mannered, and business-like members of our society. Hildy and his boss do not ring true today."

ABC took advantage of a triumphant Broadway revival of the play in 1969 and 1970—Walter Kerr's four-word lead to a lengthy Sunday appraisal in the *New York Times* was: "O Admirable *Front Page!*"—to air a ninety-minute special, complete with several members of the New York cast. Helen Hayes, MacArthur's widow who'd played a minor role during six weeks of the revival, served as narrator.

The many uses of *The Front Page* after 1928—there's even a musical version, *Windy City*, that's been produced in this country and abroad since the 1980s—attest to its longevity and continuing appeal as a sometimes faithful, sometimes fun-house reflection of press performance. Yet the play itself also proved influential to this country's stage history.

"*The Front Page* took the corsets off the American theatre, and made it possible for me to write my kind of play," Tennessee Williams once remarked. With corsets removed, it became easier to see the shape, indeed the reality, of a subject. Characters seemed drawn from life, as Williams, Arthur Miller, and other late-twentieth-century dramatists subsequently showed.

After *The Front Page*, journalism and its practitioners also came into sharper focus for the general public. Despite the play's origins—featuring a definite place with local circumstances at a particular time—the picture of newsmaking remained strikingly current and transportable beyond the city limits of Chicago.

In 1961, the French translation—*Spéciale Dernière*—became a hit in Paris, and eleven years later the National Theatre, at the urging of Laurence Olivier and Kenneth Tynan, brought *The Front Page* to the London stage, winning wide acclaim. Until 1972, although the published version had been available in England since 1929, the government there refused to grant the play a license to perform because of its profanity.

In recent years, numerous British revivals have stoked pro-con debates about tabloid news and its continuing role among national media in the United Kingdom. Last summer, for instance, the Chichester Festival Theatre outside London launched its season with *The Front Page*. "The behavior of the press doesn't vary that much when you compare yesterday to today," one cast member observed, explaining the repeated productions in Britain. This summer, in fact, London's National Theatre features John Guare's stage adaptation of *His Girl Friday*. Called "an unusual theatrical hybrid" by its producers, this rendition, a box-office success, derives from both the original play *and* the 1940 film.

Like Evelyn Waugh's novel *Scoop*, there's something intrinsically telling, farcical yet true about the portrayal of the press and its waywardness that emerges from the laughter of *The Front Page*. The characters Hecht and MacArthur brought to life by using their personal experiences have in the past seventy-five years turned into enduring stereotypes of journalism. Different times and vastly different technologies notwithstanding, the drive of news competition, the excitement of a big story, and the sense of purposeful fun still animate how journalists think, talk, and act.

The curtain never really falls on *The Front Page*.

—*Poynteronline*, August 13, 2003

PART II

Matters Literary

Although contemporary political culture and communications occupy much of my attention, I have never been able to abandon ("outgrow" might be more accurate) a teenage absorption in the writing process and specific kinds of writing. Books about authors' habits and methods crowd library shelves that should probably be devoted to more substantive volumes, while visits to used-book shops invariably lead to asking about hard-to-locate titles by Lewis Mumford or Edmund Wilson—writer-thinkers who wrote for a general readership and were in their prime during the early and middle years of the twentieth century.

Articles in this section deal with particular kinds of writing and more general literary concerns. At a time that abounds in all manner of communication, it is increasingly difficult to find successors to the public intellectuals of the past. There are some, to be sure, but our cluttered and politicized mediascape make it more difficult for them to have the common-reader and collective influence we previously saw.

The briefer, admittedly idiosyncratic essays and articles are one word-smith's response to an aspect of literary life at a given time. A fugitive idea or chance event would lead to random notes or more directed research and, somehow or other, around a thousand words would end up on a series of nearly unreadable pages. That some of these efforts try to take a reader "inside" the writing process is intentional. Although the vagaries of composition remain, by and large, mysterious, I keep trying to find words for what often seems inexplicable.

Where Have All the Thinkers Gone?

After a decade when "the egghead" was constantly ridiculed for contributing little more than hot air to Cold War America, the historian Richard Hofstadter identified "resentment and suspicion of the life of the mind" as a deeply rooted national trait in his 1963 book *Anti-Intellectualism in American Life*. This sobering study of cultural querulousness won a Pulitzer Prize, and it remains a literary landmark in pointing out a pervasive characteristic of a predominately pragmatic country.

Native wariness of the vaporously theoretical or unduly abstract made the down-to-earth, cracker-barrel philosophizing of Ben Franklin, Mark Twain, or Will Rogers indigenously more acceptable in the New World. Masking rumination with folksy wit and common sense, these "wise fools" prompted people to think—but reinforced suspicions about sophisticated cogitation.

Today, however, a contradictory concern now creates a brow-furrowing conundrum among more and more idea watchers: Who are the contemporary intellectuals best able to help the public at large think through the essential issues and problems of our time?

The recent publication of Richard A. Posner's *Public Intellectuals: A Study of Decline*—and the robust debate it initiated—posed the question anew in high-decibel fashion, drowning out anything resembling a cogent (or even tentatively satisfactory) answer. One newsmagazine report about the book inquired in stark, boldface type: "All Thought Out?"

Perturbed by the punditry intellectuals offer via the media about matters of national consequence, Posner—a federal appellate judge, law school lecturer, and prolific writer—attempted a systematic analysis of such work, complete with tables, figures, and formulas. As a scholarly study intent on delivering definitive results in a rigorously scientific way, *Public Intellectuals* is something of a guidebook for what not to do. The book, however, is useful in explaining why the current state of reflective, thought-provoking commentary and criticism for a general audience prompts questions—and criticism of its own.

Echoing Russell Jacoby's argument in *The Last Intellectuals*, which appeared in 1987 and lamented "the eclipse of public intellectuals," Posner places much of the blame on the mania for specialization that's become *de rigueur* throughout the modern university in recent decades. (For example, while political science claimed 5 subdisciplines in 1960, the number mushroomed to 104 by 2000—with more, inevitably, on the way.)

Narrowing any academic field deepens its work, as the plumbing of abstruse subjects clarifies their meaning with microscopic specificity. But this process can make resulting research and scholarship more insular, more the province of professionals communicating only among peers. Enlightening a wider public can be about the furthest consideration on a specialist's mind.

Up until the 1950s or so, independent intellectuals—men and women of ideas and letters—wrote essays and books for the intelligent yet common reader, and that work was their life and livelihood. Lewis Mumford, Edmund Wilson, Mary McCarthy, Dwight Macdonald, Hannah Arendt, and others fearlessly tackled culture, politics, and matters of the mind in accessible prose from a generalist's (rather than specialist's) point of view. They took complicated subjects—everything from the threats to civilization posed by modern technology to the Dead Sea Scrolls—and explained them in an idiom the public could comprehend.

The post–World War II growth in American higher education and the emphasis on a prosperous standard of living in the 1950s prompted formerly independent intellectuals (notably such figures as Alfred Kazin, Irving Howe, and Daniel Bell) to accept faculty positions at colleges and universities. A teaching job meant steady income, health care, and retirement benefits— and, as Bell quipped, "June, July, August and September."

Over time, though, as specialization and professionalization circumscribed academe, the broadly gauged thinker who concentrated on communicating ideas and interpretations to a general audience became about as common as a raccoon coat on the American campus. As Jacoby perceptively points out in *The Last Intellectuals*: "If the western frontier closed in the 1890s, the cultural frontier closed in the 1950s. After this decade intellectuals joined established institutions or retrained."

What happened in the intellectual realm also occurred, in parallel fashion and time frame, with literary writing. While Sinclair Lewis, Eugene O'Neill, Pearl S. Buck, William Faulkner, Ernest Hemingway, and John Steinbeck—all American recipients of the Nobel Prize for Literature during the twentieth century—steadfastly focused on their writing throughout their careers, more recent Nobel laureates (Saul Bellow in 1976 and Toni Morrison in 1993) are academics as well as authors. Even more tellingly, the expansion of creative writing programs at U.S. universities led to a continuing migration of serious novelists, poets, and dramatists to campuses.

Unlike the case of a Hemingway or Steinbeck, the security of an academic appointment means an author need not worry about the next book royalty or magazine fee to pay monthly bills. It also means a teacher-writer can publish more experimental, avant-garde work that might not appeal to the public at large. So-called "little magazines" and small presses thrive in this university-dependent climate.

Cast a cold eye at a bestseller list today, and you see mass-market novels composed by writers with definite genres—romance, mystery, thriller, espionage, and the like. It's difficult to imagine their creations being taught in future literature classes.

The reality of contemporary popular fiction offers other lessons that bear on the current state of the public intellectual. Mainstream publishers seek (and promote) novels that have a chance of blockbuster success through chain bookstore sales. Those same publishers have similar, if not quite as grand, expectations for others books, including those dealing with more cerebral concerns.

More significantly, the publishing industry is an integral part of a more encompassing entertainment and communications environment, with specific values, motivations, and ways of operating. At the same time when there's woe-is-us worry about the demise of discussion-setting public intellectuals, the media more frequently rely on their contemporary embodiment. A big story—terrorist attacks on America, a disputed national election, the impeachment investigation of a president—demands perspective and context from putatively knowledgeable sources.

In a twinkling, "experts" arrive to provide commentary and analysis on television or radio as well as throughout newspapers or magazines. Illuminating as this work can be, Posner is justified in noting that academics can, indeed, "make fools of themselves in public by writing [and talking] precipitately about matters outside their area of professional specialization." Like power and money, celebrity can corrupt—and turn a promising thinker into a dial-a-quote "publicity" intellectual.

Be that as it may, it's important to describe the situation more fully—and not just rail at the fates for work that, in Posner's view, "is becoming less distinctive, less interesting, and less important." With institutions of higher education and agenda-oriented think tanks the places intellectuals call home nowadays, obligations beyond writing and speaking for public understanding take precedence. In academe, tenure and promotion come, in large measure, from stellar teaching and specialized scholarship.

Academics who comment to the media or publish journalistic articles are, in other words, engaging in unnatural acts. And at think tanks, resident fellows or scholars tend to push particular ideological or political positions in agreement with policies espoused by the sponsoring institute or center. In either case, the affiliated nature of the intellectual can raise questions and inhibit independence. Faculty colleagues, for example, might deem such moonlighting in the limelight detrimental to a serious scholar's career. The public, by contrast, could consider such work a form of slumming, largely for ego enhancement rather than intellectual enlightenment or elevation.

Whether fair or not, these concerns conspire to make Posner, Jacoby, and other observers long for those past thinkers who saw their job as the accessible communication of ideas and their consequences to a general audience. In much the same way that the historian Daniel J. Boorstin in his 1961 book, *The Image*, identified the evolution of the mass media as a prime reason for the devolution from genuine hero to well-known celebrity, we see a similar phenomenon with intellectuals of yesterday and today. Modes of presentation play a principal role in how we assess the substance being communicated.

For much of the twentieth century, longer formats—the extended essay, the series of articles, the book—provided public thinkers with the appropriate space and context for reflective writing. Today many more potential outlets exist—in broadcasting, cable, print, the Internet—but, in most cases, they possess either conventions or requirements that aren't necessarily conducive to arguments and analysis of earlier vintage.

Some television and radio programs allow amplified, thorough airing of a subject, yet in most cases the strictures of the sound bite dictate brevity. Newspapers carry either a quotation of a couple of sentences or a 750-word opinion column, and that's pretty much it. Although magazines such as the *Atlantic Monthly*, *Harper's*, and the *New Yorker* still run thoughtful disquisitions on matters that matter, the overwhelming trend in weekly or monthly publications is to less text and to specific "niche" audiences. The book business, as noted earlier, is very much a bottom-line enterprise, fixated on potential sales of several thousand copies for any title. In short, how media operate on a day-to-day basis determines who gets attention and what form the message might take.

Moreover, the dramatic expansion in sources of communication during recent years allows everyone greater choice and more selection. This boon, however, comes at a public price—a continuing fragmentation of audiences and a marked decline in a commonly shared culture.

These days, it's less possible for public intellectuals to exert their previous influence because the methods of communications are vastly different from before, and agreement over which thinker deserves more consideration than another is more debatable because the number increases as media grow. Greater quantity doesn't insure quality, as dismissive remarks about "celebrity intellectuals" or, worse, "talking heads" imply.

In this environment of rapid change and constant exposure, there's bound to be nostalgia for an earlier time when identifying intellectuals who counted among a broader public was relatively easy. Lewis Mumford, for instance, wrote with learned authority and muscular felicity about literature, art, architecture, urban planning, technology, and numerous other subjects— with readers from his first book in 1922 until his final one six decades later expecting thoughtful guidance through thorny topics. Although he focused more exclusively on literary concerns, Edmund Wilson also enjoyed a similar reputation until his death in 1972.

Today, given the circumstances of academic or think tank affiliation along with the exigencies of popular communications, it's more difficult to single out a few unquestionably significant public intellectuals. To illustrate how crowded Posner views the field, he lists 607 names in his research. His perception of decline might derive from an absence of discrimination; however, the large number is itself a revealing fact in trying to arrive at any contemporary judgment of individual achievement.

Someone such as Garry Wills, who's held academic appointments at Johns Hopkins, Northwestern, and Notre Dame over the years, certainly qualifies as one of this country's most commanding thinkers and writers. A longtime newspaper columnist and magazine contributor, Wills has published some twenty-five books about an array of topics—political history, the Catholic Church, contemporary America, Shakespeare's *Macbeth*, the city of Venice, John Wayne, Saint Augustine, and G. K. Chesterton. Winner of the Pulitzer Prize and the National Book Critics Circle Award for *Lincoln at Gettysburg*, Wills has completed six studies of individual American presidents.

Though less prolific than Wills, Susan Sontag maintains a considerable following for her essays and books that probe cultural matters and contemporary thought. Unlike other public intellectuals today, Sontag is an independent writer, quite willing to challenge conventional wisdom. Shortly after the terrorist attacks in 2001, she received a hail of criticism for observing in the *New Yorker* that "voices licensed to follow the event [of September 11] seem to have joined together in a campaign to infantilize the public. Where is the acknowledgment that this was not a 'cowardly' attack on 'civilization' or 'liberty' or 'humanity' or 'the free world' but an attack on the world's self-proclaimed superpower, undertaken as a consequence of specific American alliances and actions? . . . And if the word 'cowardly' is to be used, it might be more aptly applied to those who kill from beyond the range of retaliation, high in the sky, than to those willing to die themselves in order to kill others."

An abundance of astute and accessible public work is currently being done by African-American academics and scholars. Henry Louis Gates Jr., Shelby Steele, bell hooks, Cornel West, Thomas Sowell, and Stephen Carter (to name a few) address racial questions as well as other issues with a general audience in mind. They are willing to look beyond the concerns of ivy-covered academe to explain the past and present in innovative ways. Gates, for instance, has made television documentaries, while West recently created a spoken-word CD, *Sketches of My Culture.*

Mentioning a few public intellectuals from a long list—even if Posner's accounting of more than six hundred seems hopelessly inflated—might seem an injustice. But, considering all the possibilities, it's easier to make the point that compelling work for an intelligent audience now involves more creators than ever before. Competition and choice discourage dominance. While the past featured easily nameable public thinkers, the field is currently so crowded it's more difficult to distinguish the heroic mind from the mere talking head.

In addition, the multitude proliferates when you gaze beyond campuses and think tanks to the practitioners of what could be called "mindful journalism." More than ever before, writers affiliated with newspapers and magazines (many having earned graduate degrees) seem willing to take on larger, public concerns in reflective, analytical ways that extend and advance their reportage. The work of Barbara Ehrenreich or David Brooks represents a journalism of social and cultural commentary that stretches the usual limits of traditional news coverage or opinion pieces. Such work also serves a purpose of combining shoe-leather reporting and serious reading of pertinent studies to produce informed, readable inquiry.

Jean Bethke Elshtain, a professor of social and political ethics in the University of Chicago's Divinity School and highly regarded author of academically grounded trade books, once cracked: "The problem with being a public intellectual is you get more and more public and less and less intellectual." Especially with the ravenous, round-the-clock media and the opportunity to speak to this conference one day and conduct a seminar for another group the next, invitations to participate publicly can themselves become obstacles to more serious and lasting projects.

In his memoir *New York Jew,* Alfred Kazin reports how Edmund Wilson used the U.S. Mail to protect himself and his time: "To ward off the many people who want something from a 'name,' he had a postcard printed up on which it was noted (with a check against the appropriate box) that Edmund Wilson does not read manuscripts for strangers; does not write articles or books to order; does not write forewords or introductions; does not make statements for publicity purposes; does not do any kind of editorial work, judge literary contests, give interviews, broadcast or appear on television; does not answer questionnaires, contribute to or take part in symposiums. And so on!"

Such self-absorption seems admirably anachronistic, a throwback to a time when (in the title of another Kazin memoir) *Writing Was Everything.* Today academic and journalistic demands on someone who engages in public work make it more difficult, if not impossible, to say "no" as a general rule to every outside request. In addition, saying "yes" can help differentiate someone from the crowd, enhancing status and recognition—to become (in a way) more like Wilson.

Although the facts of public life for an intellectual have changed in recent decades, the role such a thinker-writer plays for the nation itself remains essentially the same. Through whatever means of communication most effectively delivers perspective and insight, we look to such a figure for ideas that invigorate a democracy's discourse and decision making.

"I'm not a donkey, and I don't have a field," a respected sociologist retorted after a colleague questioned his straying from the straight-and-narrow of his defined area of scholarship. Such bold open-mindedness strikes at the heart of what serious, and successful, public intellectuals strive to do.

By abandoning the confines of a specialized discipline to seek more encompassing connections among related subjects and by presenting those findings in vigorously immediate language, public intellectuals help others see culture and society steadily and whole. For legitimate reasons, we might find fault with what some of them do, but their total eclipse—like anti-intellectualism itself—leads to nowhere but darkness.

—*Notre Dame Magazine*, Summer 2002

Postscript

The death of Susan Sontag at the end of 2004 rekindled discussion of the difficulties a thinker unattached to a university now endures in America. With publishers salivating for blockbuster titles national book chains can distribute in volume, the thoughtful exegesis of a subject or a collection of learned essays struggles to gain attention or shelf space. Such works do get published, especially by smaller presses, but a writer can't expect to make a living from their sales. Even Sontag (who once remarked: "To be a polymath is to be interested in everything—and in nothing else") turned to fiction writing with a popular audience in mind during her later years. She rhapsodized about the joy of writing novels, but she'll be remembered for her essays and criticism— and what she represented as a public thinker.

HEADNOTE

During Max Lerner's long career as a thinker, writer, and teacher, he kept discovering new ways to deliver his ideas and opinions to the public. He'd compose a longer-view essay for a highbrow journal or a glossy magazine, and then tackle yet another newspaper column about a subject of more immediate concern. At the same time, there were always courses to prepare, lecture dates to make, and books to complete.

A founder of the interdisciplinary field of American studies as well as an active journalist, he was willing to tutor a wide-eyed acolyte determined to keep one foot in the classroom and another in the newsroom. Lerner served as the inaugural W. Harold and Martha Welch Visiting Professor at the University of Notre Dame (from 1982 to 1984), where we taught together and became friends. When he died in 1992, I began work with his son, Stephen, as Max's literary executor. What happened during the next several years to finish someone else's writing projects provided the background for an essay published in the *Chicago Tribune* "Books" section in 1998.

A decade earlier, I had written two lengthy magazine pieces about Lerner, explaining his protean intellect, energetic work habits, and varied life. The article here is principally the one that appeared in the *Quill*, but some paragraphs from the second profile, published by *Notre Dame Magazine*, are added for context and elaboration.

Near the end of William F. Buckley's *New Yorker* essay-memoir about life as a public speaker, which he reprinted in *Miles Gone By: A Literary Autobiography* (2004), he writes: "The late Max Lerner, a learned evangelist, who was truly contented when instructing others how to think and what to believe in, told me that a perfect life for him would involve lecturing every day of the week: the rabbinical itch." Actually, Max loved any opportunity—via written or spoken word—to share with others what was (in his often-repeated phrase) "running through my mind."

Keeping Words Alive

Near the beginning of the biography *Max Lerner: Pilgrim in the Promised Land* (University of Chicago Press), Sanford Lakoff asserts that "no American writer in the century wrote for as many different audiences" as Max Lerner.

That compliment—for someone who produced several books (including the much-praised *America as a Civilization*) and articles that appeared everywhere from the *American Scholar* and *Foreign Affairs* to the *Ladies' Home Journal* and *Playboy*—carries with it something of a curse. Call it the curse of classification. Where do you put all those words? It's a question that has occupied more than a few hours of my time since Lerner's death in 1992.

A few weeks before he died at age eighty-nine, the two of us met at his New York apartment on the day (it turned out) he composed his last syndicated newspaper column, one of more than seven thousand he filed over a half century of part-time journalistic commentary. His eyes still danced, but more slowly and with less playfulness. Several illnesses had taken their toll and, sadly, he wanted to know: "Would you have recognized me?"

Weak and frail as he was, writing anything must have been an act of will, and (uncharacteristically) he didn't talk about the just-completed column but about the end of "a good life." In the past whenever he broached the topic of his mortality, I kept the inevitable at bay, usually with a lame remark about his indestructibility. This time, though, given his chancy condition and marked decline, I let him talk.

He mentioned book projects he'd contemplated and, in some cases, started. Could I, he wanted to know, try to complete them? More generally, would I be willing to help serve as his literary executor?

Without really understanding what might be expected or required, I agreed. How could someone who'd grown up admiring a writer's work—and had come, through fate or fortune, to know that very writer—say no?

Yet little did I realize then how the years ahead would involve words Lerner left behind. Not long after he died, I started to receive boxes with outlines of book projects, unpublished manuscripts, and other flotsam and jetsam from over six decades at the writing trade. He had also been a professor at Sarah Lawrence, Harvard, Williams, Brandeis, and Notre Dame, so there were additional piles of course descriptions and lectures with which to contend.

Amid a small forest's worth of paper, one neatly typed sheet stood out. It listed the titles of thirty books or new, updated editions of earlier volumes he hoped to finish. From what I can tell, this ambitious agenda was drawn up when Lerner was in his mid-eighties.

Many of the books on the wish list never got beyond a first chapter or a few fugitive notes. Others, happily, were far enough along that an editorial tuck and trim or some strategic reshaping could prepare them for publication.

Being a literary executor (I now know) is something of a balancing act. You need to keep up with routine requests for reprint permissions, but you also have to figure out how to present unpublished manuscripts for readers today. This can mean clarifying or cutting what at the time of writing were contemporary references. It can also mean drafting introductions and notes for context and background. You must explain why a work deserves to appear posthumously.

In the early 1940s, Lerner published *The Mind and Faith of Justice Holmes*, a popular, influential volume combining an extended biographical and analytical appraisal of Oliver Wendell Holmes Jr. with a wide selection of his most important writings. Several years later, Lerner set out to do a similar book on Thomas Jefferson.

Although the massive project of assembling Jefferson's varied prose was never completed, the messy, wrinkled, onion-skin version of the introduction I unearthed in one box seemed a perceptive primer on the man from Monticello. For a few chapters, however, closing paragraphs were either missing or, alas, had never been written. Fortunately, Lerner had discussed Jefferson at such length in other places that some reworked points from elsewhere could be cobbled together to provide suitable endings.

Was it worth it to rescue these abandoned pages and turn them into *Thomas Jefferson: America's Philosopher-King* (Transaction Publishers)? Well, the little book is in its second printing, and a historian from Jefferson's own University of Virginia remarked in a so-called learned journal that "Lerner's essay can still be read to advantage as one of the best short introductions to Jefferson currently available." The reviewer even referred to the book's editor as "Lerner's amanuensis." I've been called worse.

Since 1992, five new books "by Max Lerner" have appeared, prompting not only critical reassessments but several letters from longtime Lerner readers about what his writing meant in their lives. One went so far as to propose a documentary film about Lerner's life and work, complete with suggestions of people to interview and angles to pursue.

In assembling the most recently published volume, *Wounded Titans: American Presidents and the Perils of Power* (Arcade), I discovered that Lerner's drive to write and express himself often exceeded his desire for publication. Sorting through all the boxes, I kept finding lengthy essays about individual presidents or the presidency that had never been published.

In certain instances, a magazine or journal had rejected a piece, but there were no subsequent attempts at placement. Other essays had been composed and set aside. It's as though new projects crowded out ones completed earlier. A restless, energetic mind kept rushing forward, rarely looking back but leaving a trail of words to mark the way.

Near the end of his biography, Lakoff quotes from a diary entry Lerner jotted down in 1988, sketching out ideas for a memorial service after his death. Stephen Lerner, himself an author and my partner as literary executor, read the passage at a ceremony in his father's honor at the New School in New York: "Perhaps someone will read from stuff I have written, saying I lived for words. I shall die with some pleasure at leaving words behind, along with children and their children to recall them."

To help keep those words alive is the least a friend can do.

—*Chicago Tribune*, August 30, 1998

Never at a Loss for Words

It is approaching midnight on the East Side of New York. Max Lerner has finished a column, done some chores for a collection of essays on the U.S. Constitution, and now there's time to talk. He muses aloud about the vagaries of politics and column writing.

In the early 1970s, Lerner was high on Richard Nixon's "Enemies List." But recently, Lerner got a call from John Taylor, one of Nixon's assistants. Taylor said that Nixon had asked him to pass this along to Lerner: "He [Nixon] was talking with President Reagan the other day and said, 'Ron, have you read Max Lerner this morning?' And President Reagan said, 'Yes, I've read him, Dick. I always read Max Lerner.'"

Times—and people—change. What Lerner writes today is recommended reading by the former president and a steady diet for the current president.

Lerner, eighty-five, is the oldest of the national columnists. He estimates that in the past forty-five years he has filed over seven thousand columns for *PM* (a short-lived liberal paper in New York, founded in 1940 by Chicago's Marshall Field); for the *New York Post*; and, for the past two decades, for the Los Angeles Times Syndicate.

Seven *thousand* columns. "It's a shattering thought," he admits. "But coming up with subjects has never been difficult. My problem has always been that I have too many topics crying to be tackled."

Lerner calls writing a regular column a "strange necessity," the phrase English novelist and critic Rebecca West once used to refer to the craft of writing. Although he has occasionally thought about abandoning journalistic commentary in order to concentrate on books and longer articles, he finds it impossible to stop.

He has managed to slow down a bit, though. In the late 1950s, he went from writing four columns a week to three. A couple of years ago, he decided to cut down to two a week.

Since the 1930s, Lerner has bridged the worlds of journalism and scholarship. Before becoming editorial director of *PM* in 1943, he was an editor of *The Encyclopedia of the Social Sciences* and a professor at Sarah Lawrence College, Harvard University, and Williams College in Massachusetts. He also had edited the *Nation* and contributed frequently to the *New Republic*.

"My academic work is critical to my journalistic writing," he says. "I also feel, as an academic, that I don't want to write for just a coterie of my fellow professors. The 'public intellectual'—one who tries to reach the general public—has almost disappeared from university life. The public discourse would be better with his return."

Lerner currently divides his time between New York State, where he has a Manhattan apartment and a Southampton summer home, and California, where he teaches human behavior at the graduate school of U.S. International University in San Diego.

As a self-proclaimed "civilization watcher," he finds the bicoastal life an asset to both writing and teaching. Since 1949, Lerner has commuted from New York to three universities where he has been a professor. He taught at Brandeis University in Boston from 1949 to 1973, and he joined the faculty of U.S.I.U. in 1974. From 1982 to 1984, he taught American studies at the University of Notre Dame in Indiana.

Lerner has commented on almost every imaginable subject related to political and social affairs—from the evils of fascism to the dangers of detente; from the dominance of liberal thinking to the rise of the Reagan era of conservatism; from Alfred Kinsey's earliest studies of the sexual behavior of men and women to the more recent sexual backlash caused by the threat of sexually transmitted diseases, including AIDS. His principal beat, however, has been the ideas that influence how people think and act.

"I suspect that what really counts in history, along with great leaders, is ideas," Lerner says. "Commentators tend to be cheerleaders or the leaders of the damning crowd. I don't like either role for myself.

"If we serve a function, it ought to be one beyond cheerleading and damning. We should act as a bridge between those shaping ideas and the expression of them in the political arena."

Martin Peretz, the editor in chief of the *New Republic,* has followed Lerner's columns since the early 1950s. He believes that only two journalists—Lerner and the late Walter Lippmann—have been what he calls "journalists of ideas." Lippmann may appear to have been more important, Peretz says, but that importance lay in Lippmann's personal relationships to power.

"I think that if an anthropologist of ideas, 50 years hence, looks back at these two careers, the Lerner corpus will be much more impressive—and much less wrong," Peretz says.

Born in Russia, Mikhail Lerner immigrated to the United States in 1907 at age four. Arriving at New York's Ellis Island, he was given the first name of Max because, his parents were told, "You can't call a Jewish boy by an Irish name, Michael."

As a war correspondent for *PM* in 1945, he saw Europe in rubble, but his thoughts turned to his adopted country. Surveying the ruins, he says that he "couldn't help thinking of Gibbon and the ruins of Rome. I thought 'What's happened here to the history of Western civilization?'

"Then it hit me that America is a civilization in its own right, distinct from Europe, and that I wanted to spend the rest of my life figuring out what lies ahead for American civilization."

During the 1950s, with academic specialization on the rise, Lerner took the considerable intellectual risk of trying to survey all aspects of American life and thought in a single volume. *America as a Civilization* appeared in 1957, earning critical acclaim as a work that followed in the tradition of two classic nineteenth-century studies—Alexis de Tocqueville's *Democracy in America* and James Bryce's *The American Commonwealth.* The book sold more than one hundred thousand copies and was translated into eight languages. A thirtieth-anniversary edition was published in 1987, with an added chapter about "The New America: 1957–1987."

Surveying the past three decades, Lerner takes issue with thinkers who believe the country is in decline or, even worse, dying. He acknowledges that America has suffered "scarring experiences"—like the Vietnam War and Watergate—but he views these wounds to the body politic as "the turmoils of adolescence" rather than signs of a terminal condition. "Compared with the historic civilizations which have lasted for millennia—China, India, Russia, Europe—America is still a stripling," he writes, "with almost everything ahead of it to experience and suffer, but caught . . . between the responsibilities of power and the dreams and excesses of youth."

With his academic background and his emphasis on ideas, Lerner probably relies on books more than most columnists do. "Reading for me is a source bed," he notes. "Without it you don't have a frame. Of course, experience counts most, but you need to put the experience into the frame of what has been transmitted over the centuries by people who have tried to figure out what their experience meant."

Given his belief in the primacy of the polity, Lerner is strongly president-oriented. He has talked with every president since Franklin Roosevelt except Ronald Reagan. (Illness prevented him from keeping an appointment with Reagan.)

"What I tried to carry away from each conversation was not a 'scoop,' but quite simply a fuller context for the president's actions—a sense of the connection between what I saw in them vividly, face-to-face, and their public persona and decision-making. To some extent, my visits were—to use that barbarous term—psychohistorical visits."

Lerner says that he was looking for some continuity in their lives, some link between their character and the way they met crises. Walter Lippmann and Theodore H. White practiced that kind of journalism, too, he says, but reflective commentary is being pushed out of the op-ed pages today in favor of what he calls "the immediacy stuff."

Lerner also thinks that some of the current columnists have a narrow viewpoint that makes what they write predictable. Although he has generally scorned labels for himself, Lerner felt he had to live with the label "liberal columnist" for the first two decades of writing newspaper commentary. During the 1930s and early 1940s, his praise of collectivism, coupled with his critique of capitalism, had led American communists to woo him. He rejected their overtures, saying, "I have never been a soldier in anyone's political army, and I never will be."

Following the publication of his *America as a Civilization,* he spent a lengthy period abroad to write *The Age of Overkill: A Preface to World Politics* (1962). His discussions with foreign leaders and his travels on every continent marked a turning point in his thinking.

"I began to see that the liberal dynamism of what I now call 'social engineering' was not healthy for America," Lerner says. "I moved *away* from my earlier sense that some kind of socialized economy and human engineering society was what I wanted. My viewpoint shifted. I no longer thought of myself as a liberal. But I have never thought of myself as a conservative, either.

"What counts in any society is whether it has a center and whether the center holds. In this sense, Yeats proves to be the best political thinker: 'Things fall apart; the center cannot hold.' My prime question now is whether the center holds in the midst of tumultuous and abrasive change."

Lerner was interviewed recently by William F. Buckley Jr. on *Firing Line.* Buckley challenged him about his shift of view. Lerner responded that he regards himself as a "radical centrist."

"I feel the only really radical angle of vision is one that gets at the root of the problem," Lerner said. "Whatever counts most in any problem you're approaching must be sought at the very center of it, where the polar opposites meet."

To examine this center, he says, one needs historical context. Julie Farkas, Lerner's editor at the Los Angeles Times Syndicate, notes, "There's an old line: We learn nothing from history except that we learn nothing from history. Well, Max *has* learned. He knows what went before. He sees the cyclical swings in civilizations. His historical approach makes him different from other columnists today."

Beginning with his columns in the 1960s, Lerner has focused on cycles in values. "The essence of a culture," he says, "rests on the values it not only professes—but lives. Their source is in economic, sexual and religious life. Every generation fights over them, in every decade. From the start of the century to the present, there are strong signs of action, recoil, and return in a three-decade cycle."

But Lerner doesn't just look backward. He has at least one eye on the future. When he considers potential subjects for columns, he asks himself whether the topic has enough lasting significance to interest readers in years to come.

"One test I've always used is to ask whether in 10, 15, or 20 years the piece will still stand up. Journalism need not be evanescent. I've broken sharply with many of my working newspaper friends who have felt 'this is today's story; there'll be another tomorrow, and still another the day after.' For me, journalism is for today and tomorrow, yes. But you hope that some of it will last beyond changes and fashions."

Lerner has collected several hundred of his columns in three volumes, *Public Journal* (1945), *Actions and Passions* (1949), and *The Unfinished Country* (1959). During the next few years, he plans to put together collections that draw from columns written in the 1960s through the 1980s.

"We're not in the business of writing classics," he says of commentators. "But some of our stuff ought to give characteristic shape to each decade."

Asked about early influences, people who might have helped shape his own career, Lerner picks three writers. "I came of age in the early '20s," he recalls, "when the Pulitzer-owned *New York World* was my meat and drink. It had two contrasting columnists. When Heywood Broun was good, as he was on Sacco and Vanzetti, he was incomparable. He was pithy and witty, and his danger was a kind of moral absolutism. But it gave his columns punch."

The other columnist that Lerner admired was William Bolitho, a South African who lived in France and wrote columns "in the Montaigne tradition—wide-ranging, reflective little essays built around symbols, like his famous one on 'Clemenceau's bands.'"

Later, Lerner says, in the thirties, Walter Lippmann became a model he accepted "only reluctantly, because I opposed most of his positions. Yet I was drawn to his magisterial style, even when I found it a bit pompous and arrogant.

"In the end, whatever your influences, you fashion your own style."

On column-writing days, Mondays and Wednesdays, Lerner reviews his notebook entries to pick a topic.

"You watch for the something that makes a column become an entity," he says. "At a certain point I can say: 'This is what makes it mine.' All week long there is a scarcely-conscious process—a confluence of what's happening in the news and what's happening in my mind.

"The news is a starting point. When it meets something I've been brooding over for weeks or months, then a column idea is born."

Then, he says, he is like a dog with something to gnaw on. "The rest is a lot of work and sweat—and a little bloodletting. But it's play, too. The way the idea develops, its phrasing, can surprise you so that you yelp because you've found the right phrase, sentence, ending."

Lerner says that his columns are less abrasive and confrontational than they were in earlier years. "I hope a reader sees me in the process of trying to face something," he says. "Generally, my earlier ones were about the conclusion I had reached. Now I try to lay bare my process.

"Every column has to be an adventure in recovery and possibility," he says. "I like best the ones that send me back over the years—to people and places I had almost forgotten, to ideas I picked up somewhere and have made my own.

"Every column is a ransacking of your mind, a plunge into deeper waters than you expected when you started. And every column is a discovery of things you didn't know you were thinking. That's what brings its surprises."

Lerner spends two to three hours working up notes and three hours writing each column. He paces himself to finish at the last possible moment for the syndicate to send it to his approximately sixty subscribing papers. "I am a champion of deadlines," he says. "Deadlines make the mind race; they make the words and phrases come quicker. Almost all of my columns are best at the end, because that is where the pressure and tension mount to a catharsis of sorts."

That rush, the exhilaration Lerner gets from writing, has become a lifesaving resource. In 1980, doctors discovered an advanced lymphoma and gave him six months to live. He beat the prognosis.

In 1982, he developed prostate cancer and, in 1984, he suffered a heart attack. He credits medical treatment with only part of his recoveries. Work has been his elixir.

"The column was one of the things that saved my life," he says. "During those years of really critical illness, I would get out of intensive care in the hospital and my wife, Edna, who knew me, would have a pen ready for me. I'd start writing my column right out of surgery. In a sense, it was the affirmation by which I conquered the cancers. It was my way of saying to the adversary, 'Do your worst. I'm alive.'"

Lerner, who has written or edited fifteen books, is currently completing a memoir about his illness, *Wrestling with the Angel*. While he was coping with the cancers, he wrote over four hundred pages of an autobiography, *Delight of Battle*, which covers the first half of his life.

In four and a half decades as a columnist, Lerner has seen countless changes in journalism. He is particularly struck by the opening up of editorial and op-ed pages to a wider array of commentators.

"Whatever comes into our lives in this democratic culture, we try to democratize," he says. "We democratize sex. We democratize suspense stories, so that now everybody is writing suspense stories. Well, why not everybody writing columns?"

When Lerner started his career in journalism, there were "a scarce dozen columnists. Now there are scores, and op-ed pages are open to outsiders. The field, however, is never too crowded for someone to stand out who has something to say.

"It is crowded in the sense that every op-ed editor now has far more available than he can use. That's not a bad situation. It means we have to earn our pay. It means we're being tested constantly against others. There are no safe jobs. If my talents and ideas can't stand up against the youngsters, well, that's it, in a free market of ideas."

Lerner would like to see greater attention to probing, in-depth commentary instead of "chatter about who's up and who's down, who's liberal, who's conservative at a given time." Perhaps, he says, the superficiality is caused by the education many journalists get.

"Journalism is one of the humanities; it's not just a trade or a vocation," he says. "The failure to mirror the richness, complexity, and interconnectedness of American life—its variability, its contradictions, its polarities—lies with the professors who have educated the journalists and, in turn, with *their* professors. What we need is a constant cross-fertilization from every discipline to every discipline."

Lerner studied literature at Yale, graduating in 1923. He then shifted to economics and constitutional law. He received an M.A. at Washington University in St. Louis in 1925 and a Ph.D. in 1927 from the Robert Brookings

Graduate School of Economics and Government in Washington, D.C. He says that journalists need a stronger concentration on rigorous courses of inquiry that provide a frame for both reporting and commentary.

In his foreword to *Public Journal*, his first collection of columns, Lerner argues that a commentator should help the reader "see America whole." To do that, a journalist needs to become broadly gauged, willing to tackle the varied themes that offer perspective on contemporary life.

"For better or worse," Lerner says, "we are all civilization-watchers. I have made it part of my job to watch America. I watch the things that are being said and done in terms of the light they shed on the civilization. When I read something, or when I note something in my daily life, I ask, 'What does it show about human beings and the society they live in? What does it show about the culture, and in the largest terms about our civilization?'

"What engages me most are the questions of how vulnerable we are as a civilization, how sick, how healthy, how enduring? How do we handle and resolve a crisis? After some major blunder like Vietnam or Watergate, how do we call upon the resources and resilience in the civilization to make it become whole again? To get at the contemporary dynamics of our existing civilization involves getting as much light as possible from the history and experience of earlier ones."

Lerner's own broad gauge as a writer makes readers see him as a generalist, a perception he doesn't mind. "A generalist is a fence jumper and boundary-crosser. He's a smuggler. He smuggles ideas across borders, but he is also constantly a synthesizer, who puts together whatever he can grasp into something that comes to life as an integrated idea," he says.

"I used to rail a good deal against specialization. But I no longer do, because I've come to believe that with the proliferation of disciplines and their fragmentation—especially in the hard sciences and the life sciences—unless you are a specialist you're not going to be able to master what you need to know. I've come to believe that it isn't an either/or dichotomy between specialism and generalism. What it is really is the difference between a specialist who remains narrow and never crosses the rivers and the boundaries, and one who—knowing his specialty—is constantly crossing them."

Journalism is only one facet of Lerner's life. In his mid-eighties, he continues to lead "five lives which intertwine." Besides turning out his syndicated column, he writes books and magazine articles, teaches, delivers lectures on the national speaking circuit, and conducts an active family and social life in both New York and California.

A typical day includes reading—books, newspapers, journals, and magazines—and watching some television news. Most of the time, though, he's writing. When not working on a specific piece, he's constantly making entries in notebooks and diaries. Confessing he's "the most disorderly man you can imagine," Lerner uses the notebooks and diaries to organize his thoughts and work out ideas. The jottings frequently become the building blocks of his writing projects and classroom presentations.

Edna Lerner calls her husband of nearly fifty years "a total worker" as well as "a wonderful father." She remembers him using a tree stump as a desk on a beach in Jamaica to write sections of *America as a Civilization*. A favorite picture of hers, taken in the 1950s and now hanging in the hallway of their Manhattan apartment, shows Lerner composing at the typewriter while one of their sons plays with his father's feet.

"He's always working," she says. "He sleeps slightly late, gets up and starts working. He works with his secretary a bit, but most of the time he's writing. He works all day, with an interruption just for dinner. We have dinner and talk, but right after dinner he starts working again, and he often works until 2 in the morning. It really is an obsessive push now."

"There is a considerable observing ego in me," he admits. "I watch myself as I work and live, and I use my diary and notebooks to keep track of what's happening in my mind and life. Edna's rather amused by this. She thinks it is my obsession with myself. My answer is: I don't know of any productive working thinker who hasn't been self-obsessed. It goes with the territory. There used to be a remark about how the stockyards in Chicago processed everything except the squeak. In a sense I too make use of everything in my life except the squeak—and sometimes even the squeak."

Above all, Lerner strives for integrative thinking, what he calls "a sense of the whole." He considers what he does "an adventure in ideas" and a "search," but he distinguishes it from what academics refer to as "research": "Research is to do it—whatever it might be—again. Those who don't do it originally do it again, so they become researchers. For me it's search; it's inquiry. You study the great thinkers and their lives to see how they went at it. You contrive in some way to get at it yourself. You wrestle with it.

"It's a little like Jacob wrestling with the angel of God. He finds in the morning that the angel has left a mark upon his thigh. This is the working thinker. He is wrestling all the time, and he gets wounded in the process. It's the wrestling, the Greek *agon*, that counts. You wrestle with every preceding figure. You wrestle with your models, to overcome them—but even more to become yourself, with them within you."

This metaphorical wrestling entails a personal, inner battle to come up with new insights and with the *mot juste* expressions for them. Work and play constantly converge. "I'm in an almost continuous state of excitement," he admits. "Edna calls it 'compulsive euphoria,' and it's the phrase of hers that's truest of me."

In Lerner's view, the current information and communication revolutions create "new symbolic environments" that deserve close scrutiny. He is particularly interested in the immediacy of news coverage now possible because of the technological capabilities of television, and in the expanded possibilities for computer delivery of information—to news organizations and into the home.

"In a sense," he says, "nothing has really happened until the media have noted it. It's like the philosophical conundrum as to whether the sound of a tree falling in the wilderness is a reality or not, when there is no one to listen to it. The same is true of events in the civilization. Unless the media present them with some emphasis, they're not events. That's the sense in which the media are the signature of the civilization."

Lerner says that he is fascinated—as an observer—with new media forms. "They have meant a revolution in world history as staggering as print was. There is nothing like the combined power of word, voice, facial expression, gesture.

"Yet my own gut loyalty has remained with print—what Marshall McLuhan called 'The Gutenberg Galaxy.' The print media, with their words and ideas, ignite the fires of great changes. The electronic media feed and fuel them.

"I am impressed with the Dickensian power of TV to reveal the underside of life, its injustices and inequalities, and to stir our conscience about righting them.

"It's a revolutionary power," he continues. "Yet I miss the full richness of words and ideas on TV. Its symbols, taken by themselves, remain one-dimensional. You still see in your memory the racks of skulls on the Cambodian killing fields. Yet they fail to convey the multiple meanings of who and what were responsible, how it happened, and most of all, how it was humanly possible. That is left for print somehow to add, with its richness of language, its texture of thought, its evocation of what is common to the intellectual tradition."

Lerner recalls a lunch with Marshall McLuhan, after McLuhan had had a stroke and shortly before he died. "His face was eager, his eyes shone, but he couldn't utter the words he wanted. . . . There was pathos in it."

What irony there is here, Lerner is saying: "Here was the great seer of communication, the man above all who had devoted his life to 'understanding media,' as his book was called, and he couldn't communicate, couldn't make his meaning clear.

"Looking back, there is more than a whiff of the symbolic in it—but in reverse. This marvelous complex of science, technology, organization and human talent that we call the media—it is capable of transmitting so cleverly, so much, so brilliantly. Yet when it comes to the meanings and insights that cry out to be communicated, they don't come through."

Because of the power of the media, Lerner believes that people both inside and outside of journalism have to be media watchers. They have to evaluate "what the media are picking as notable, whom they select to comment on events, and what they say." In reading the press and watching television, he also finds himself asking, "What *wasn't* picked, and why? What difference does that make?"

Lerner is critical of the current preoccupation with stories about crime and violence by some newspapers and local television stations. Sensational coverage, presented primarily for the emotional impact of the moment, he believes, leads to a "fragmenting of journalism and of society as well." Instead of addressing the continuities of life, this kind of journalism places undue emphasis on individual incidents.

Lerner is impressed, however, with the commitment a growing number of newspapers, such as the *Los Angeles Times* and the *Wall Street Journal*, have made to an extended treatment of critical topics. He also finds lengthy, one-on-one interviews on CNN, ABC's *Nightline*, and PBS's *NewsHour* valuable in taking the measure of public figures. "I see the potential," he says. "I am not down on journalism.

"You cannot expect journalism to be deeper or better than the larger political culture. You cannot hope that the media culture will achieve heights and depths that the political culture is too narrow and too rigid to allow."

After forty-five years of column writing, Max Lerner feels the same emotions today as when he began. "The first column I wrote," he recalls, "was for *PM*, when I joined it on a trial basis in 1943. It was on the Casablanca conference of the Allied war leaders. Ending a staff meeting, John P. Lewis [then the paper's chief] said, 'The Professor will try the edit. It will either run or it won't.'

"I was scared—but it ran.

"Am I still scared?" he asks with a laugh. "A little each time. You never know when it will lay an egg. Would I give it up? Not for the world. I can't imagine being without it. Who can be so lucky as to have this for 45 years?

"Besides, how else would I try to make sense of this crazy and incredible world? And how else would I be able to read the next day the printed version of the sense or nonsense I made of it the day before?

"Probably right up until the day I die, I will have written a column. The joy is still there, and the strange necessity. My heart leaps up when I behold the fresh print and the byline attached to it."

Lerner plans to devote his energy in future years primarily to completing books. Unlike classes and lectures, books are enduring contributions to what he calls "the memory bank of the culture." Taking the longer view at his own career with critical self-detachment, he does wonder if he should have concentrated on writing books instead of putting so much effort into his newspaper column.

"I had a chance in 1957, with the publication of *America as a Civilization*, to direct my life into a single channel, doing a new book every few years. Each book would have tried to give my political and life perspective at the time. I could by this time have had a dozen books of that kind. In terms of public perception, I think I would have emerged as a clearer figure than now. I would not have confused my audiences, who tend to ask which am I—a journalist or a long-range thinker? They wonder why I spread myself all over the intellectual map. It's a serious question I have about my life."

But Max Lerner doesn't talk much about roads not taken. There are deadlines to meet and planes to catch. As for the future, he cites a remark of Justice Holmes: "As life is action and passion, it is required of man that he should share the passion and action of his time at peril of being judged not to have lived."

He repeats the last words, "at peril of being judged not to have lived," then pauses for a moment. "I have lived, but there are still passions, reflections, insights, actions ahead. I don't know how far. I know only that I want to die young, at as advanced an age as I can stretch it to. Meanwhile there are love and work. If you can't love you die. And the final comment on work will be found in John, 'Work . . . while it is day: for the night cometh, when no man can work.'"

> —*The Quill*, November 1988, and
> *Notre Dame Magazine*, Autumn 1988

HEADNOTE

The next nine essays appeared in the "Books" section of the *Chicago Tribune* over a five-year period and treat various aspects of writing and reading. Republishing them together in chronological sequence might suggest there was a plan behind their composition. That, though, was never the case. Each essay came about on its own—and the number just grew over time, complete (alas) with a repetition here and there. Several took shape during sojourns abroad, when the tendency is to look at everything, including one's self, with a fresh-eyed perspective.

Pride and Joy

Truman Capote, who knew a thing or two about murder from writing *In Cold Blood*, once remarked, "Finishing a book is just like you took a child out in the yard and shot it."

I have a less sanguinary, more paternalistic view. To be sure, delivering a manuscript to a publisher triggers the gamut of authorial postpartum emotions—everything from ecstasy to abandonment. But once you see the typescript of a ream of loose pages transformed into a printed and bound creation—attired in a stylish jacket—you behold a literary offspring to which you will always be attached. And not just forevermore, but for better or worse.

As with children, each book will have a life of its own, an unknown destiny no one but a blockhead would dare foretell. It's possible a new arrival will be proclaimed a prodigy, dazzling everyone along the way. Alas, the opposite reception is also possible, making an author brood at the prospects for this addition to the family.

The stages of a book's life history follow their own curious, unpredictable path. Early on, reviewers christen the work in distinctive, often unceremonious ways. Unlike members of the clergy, these opinionated souls are rarely shy about pointing out warty blemishes as well as distinguishing beauty marks during these baptismal rites.

Although praise increases pride and lingers in one's memory, discouraging words can provoke what the critic Malcolm Cowley called "nightmares at noonday." How could someone, anyone, say that about something it took so much effort to produce?

Bruised by intemperate reaction or not, the book knows no better, and—truth be told—neither does the author. The work's existence is more absorbing. Featured shelf space in a bookstore is akin to prime real estate, and writers from time to time reposition a volume so the cover (rather than the much slimmer spine) is easily visible for all to admire. When a bookstore arranges an autographing party to announce a new citizen in the republic of letters, well, that's more than a stranger's pat on the head. It's a celebratory elixir to offset the solitude of incubation. Like reviews, however, such occasions are not always peak, triumphal experiences for a book and its author. Try as I might, I can't seem to forget one signing at a mall, where fascination over the free refreshments exceeded interest in the new book by a factor of fifty.

Once the flush of arrival subsides, a book is pretty much on its own. Some make their way in the world by being selected by reading clubs. Others find temporary residence in a college classroom as an assigned text. Still others, though, never seem to stray too far from home. Seemingly unappreciated and sadly unloved by other people, these books can occupy a special place in a writer's heart. In literary life, authorial favoritism usually means that readers, for one reason or another, failed to recognize qualities of a book only the writer knows—the challenges posed, the phrases turned. So it goes.

Some hardy, adventurous books travel well beyond their native grounds to far-off climes the author only dreams about visiting. You can but shake your head in wonder on learning that the telephone connection to India for the radio program about your book might be chancy because a cyclone struck just a few hours ago. And then there's the unalloyed delight of opening a (usually battered) package from afar with the translation of a book in some inscrutable language, such as Arabic or Japanese. At that point, royalties from the mysterious "subsidiary rights" become secondary to elation at knowing that people in distant lands with different cultures could find value in a book you shaped.

The New York journalist Murray Kempton, justly acclaimed for the prose artistry of his columns, took considerable satisfaction from imagining young people riding the subway randomly picking up a castoff newspaper and being moved by what he'd written. Maybe, just maybe, these words of commentary will spur someone to learn more and to do more, he thought as he wrote.

That sentiment—of possibly having influence on an unknown reader, young or old—gathers greater meaning with the permanence of a book, as you envision a volume sitting on a library shelf, waiting to be plucked down. With a perpetuity the author will never enjoy, a book will continue to live for anyone to peruse.

In "Why the Novel Matters," D. H. Lawrence wrote, "The novel is the one bright book of life." A much less inspired wordsmith might try to embellish the remark. Every book has a life of its own that's nearly always bright. At least in the eyes of its creator.

—*Chicago Tribune*, November 16, 1997

A Sentence to Write

Maybe it's a matter of age. Not so many years ago, I'd approach a new or un-finished writing project and the desk on which it sat with the trepidation of a criminal summoned to the judge's bench to receive a prison sentence.

Today, a few books and a trunk full of articles later, it's different. Now my most dreaded fear (to torture the felonious analogy) is that a court somewhere will convict me for some low crime or misdemeanor and punish me with a lengthy term in jail without access to paper and pencils.

For someone hooked on the writing habit, even Descartes requires revi-sion. The French philosopher's signature reflection, "I think, therefore I am," only proves valid by replacing "write" for "think."

To claim, "I write, therefore I am," might sound a chest-puffing scrib-bler's boast, something Ernest Hemingway at his machismo worst might bray to a barroom assemblage. But embedded in the line exists a certain truth. For many wordsmiths, present company included, the physical act of stringing one word after another leads to rumination. As E. M. Forster wisely cracked, "How do I know what I think until I see what I say?"

Famous authors, blessed with blockbuster contracts and bestseller stat-ure, are often asked—as they hawk their literary wares in media interviews—whether they write for themselves or for an amorphous, mass audience. Some piously proclaim they attend to the siren song of their respective muses for the sake of their Art, always with a capital "A." Others, attentive to more down-to-earth and bankable concerns, voice the importance of appealing to their devoted readers in imaginative yet familiar ways.

Though truthful to a point, each response dodges a preeminent reason many people prefer the monastic solitude of composition for certain periods every day: playing with words turns into a can't-help-it affliction. You write, quite simply, because you feel you need to write. And when you're not working on a specific project, you're making notes for a future linguistic wrestling match.

To rattle on like an old car about a so-called drive runs the risk of sounding egotistical, or monotonous, or (heaven forfend) both. But writing of the can't-help-it variety is—truth be told—more humbling than heartening, largely because it so often seems impossible to write something right: clearly, fully, engagingly.

Even for experienced phrasemakers, the high anxiety of a low-grade writer's block is a common malady, compounding the humility. Each blank page or screen becomes simultaneously daunting and taunting, a nagging invitation to make the effort to produce prose that at the end appears effortless.

Worrying how to fix a clumsy sentence or what move to make to continue a piece can cause something akin to an authorial trance. You can be just about anywhere else, but really at work. As James Thurber, stylist extraordinaire for the *New Yorker* at midcentury, once told an interviewer: "I never quite know when I'm not writing. Sometimes my wife comes up to me at a party and says, 'Dammit, Thurber, stop writing.' She usually catches me in the middle of a paragraph."

That sense of never being off-duty can lead to memorable moments. How could I forget stretching out in the bathtub of a motel room early one morning to scribble away, as wife and son blissfully snoozed just outside the door?

Or the time the final paragraphs of a difficult-to-end essay arrived, unannounced, near the end of a harrowing horseback ride? To this day the cowboy guide at the front must wonder what the urbanized tenderfoot bringing up the rear was doing. Scrawling out a will, he no doubt thought.

Is it a cardinal sin to occasionally jot down notes during less-edifying sections of a Sunday sermon? If so, I hereby confess and pray forgiveness.

This self-imposed sentence to write might strike some readers as a self-made psychosis, requiring professional counseling or (at the very least) participation in a support group. On the contrary, this quirky addiction brings a welcome centrality and continuity to life that's mind-clearingly therapeutic

in itself. Worrisome obsessions somehow become more manageable when reduced to words on paper.

"I have always been in a condition in which I cannot not write," the lu-
minous historian Barbara Tuchman once remarked. For some of us, that condition comes later, as hair grays and legs begin to wobble. Regardless of time
of arrival, this strange necessity, with its terrors and triumphs, knows no
remedy.

And for some equally strange and mysterious reason, tomorrow's effort at
composition always promises to be better than the one abandoned today.

—Chicago Tribune, February 8, 1998

Rites of Writing

About a year ago, as credits for the movie *As Good As It Gets* began to roll, I turned to my wife and remarked of the ostentatiously quirky writer Melvin Udall—played to Oscar-winning neurotic perfection by Jack Nicholson—"He seems weird, but that's closer to the way it is than most people think."

Her quick, pained nod of recognition silently said, "How well I know." Yes, art—even of the blockbuster Hollywood variety—can not only imitate life but also provide a glimpse into the human psyche. In this case, with Nicholson's portrayal, we see the generic individualism of anyone committed to putting words on a page.

Singularity extends both to daily interaction with the outside world and to habits of literary composition. As the film cleverly depicts, there's a public dimension to a writer's private life coexisting with intensely private sessions that lead to work for the public to behold.

Ironic inversion of public and private aside, the actual wrestling with a muse (or demon) provokes its own type of fascination. Behind every book is an untold story about how the author struggled to create and complete the book. And—to paraphrase Dr. Johnson—none but a blockhead did, indeed, struggle in the process.

Here's where the often eccentric personal rituals come into play. Over time the solitary, long-haul nature of book writing incubates idiosyncrasies that, in their curious, enigmatic way, establish an author's routine.

Although nonwriters (let us pray they are readers) might envy the stay-at-home freedom most writers enjoy, a life without rules means you're forced to create your own along the way. Will you work early in the day or late at night? How will you write—by hand (pen or pencil) or via machine (computer or typewriter)? What will you set as a day's goal, and will you measure that in a quota of words or an amount of time?

All of these individual decisions lead to the peculiar discipline a writer needs to maintain. Moreover, authors discover personal tricks that help them through the wordy silence of composition. On the C-SPAN program *Booknotes*, host Brian Lamb regularly inquires about his guest's methods and habits. Responses always prove intriguing and become approaches worth considering by other writers.

Well, maybe I should use an antique ink-dip pen, like Southern author Shelby Foote, to slow down my scribbling, which for years I've done exclusively in pencil: one specific, mechanical pencil, to be sure. Or maybe I should write in the nude, as historian Forrest McDonald says he does. On second thought, maybe not.

By focusing on how authors set words down, the first volume of Lamb's edited transcripts of *Booknotes* takes its place next to the several collections of *Paris Review* interviews in the *Writers at Work* series. Since first appearing in the late 1950s, these extended question-and-answer sessions (with the likes of William Faulkner, Ernest Hemingway, Katherine Anne Porter, Ralph Ellison, Nelson Algren, Saul Bellow, Maya Angelou, and Tom Wolfe) have helped readers—and other writers—better understand the prosy nuts and bolts of the creative process.

In his interview, Hemingway explains the essence of his technique. "If it is any use to know it, I always try to write on the principle of the iceberg. There is seven-eighths of it underwater for every part that shows. Anything you know you can eliminate and it only strengthens your iceberg. It is the part that doesn't show. If a writer omits something because he does not know it then there is a hole in the story."

How Hemingway reached the point of the visible one-eighth remains a subject of continuing captivation, witness the current multimedia hoopla surrounding the centenary of his birth in Oak Park. Although fame destructively enlarged an already outsized ego, Hemingway usually talked about his craft in ways that left a lasting impact.

It's why, truth be told, I compose in pencil. It's also why I try to keep any piece of writing a parade of relatively short, everyday words, even efforts for so-called scholarly publication.

When I happened to be in Idaho recently, I made a point of going to Ketchum to find the house where Hemingway worked the last years of his life. Repeatedly told the home was down a private road posted with "No Trespassing" signs, I persisted until a local resident (and acquaintance of one of Papa's sons) said, "If it means that much, we can probably sneak out there before you leave tomorrow."

Why it meant that much, I'm not sure. But there we were, at dawn's first light, peering in the windows of the rooms on the first floor and admiring the majestic setting above the Wood River, which snakes through the nearby mountains. Now owned by the Nature Conservancy, the house (appropriately for the previous occupant, if not the one now) sports several game heads on the living room walls.

Like reading an interview on a writer's methods or studying the authors-at-work photographs in *Booknotes* or Jill Krementz's engrossing *The Writer's Desk*, the Ketchum adventure was a chance to peek behind an author's words and see where he composed his last words. For the quirk-afflicted, learning as much as possible about the mysterious obsessions of writers becomes therapeutic self-assurance. Maybe I'm normally abnormal in how I deal with a blank page.

Knowing everything one can about the esoteric inevitability of the writing process serves a useful purpose. In our one-size-fits-all American culture, writers—like the Nicholson character in *As Good As It Gets*—stand apart, nursing their peculiarities and minding their habits.

Yet, for any author, the results of the daily jousts with the language, the published books themselves, matter most—especially whether they endure or not. As A. J. Liebling, a noted stylist and nose-flattening critic, once confessed, "The only way to write is well and how you do it is your own damn business."

—*Chicago Tribune,* June 27, 1999

Once Is Not Enough

When Joseph Heller died in late 1999, obituary writers pointed out that his intriguing book title (and enduring phrase to describe the vagaries of modernity) *Catch-22* came into being by chance—and publisher-dictated necessity.

Originally, Heller planned to call his surrealistic yet somehow true-to-life story "Catch-18." But 18 had already been taken, so to speak, by author Leon Uris for *Mila-18*, a novel based on the Warsaw uprising during World War II. To reduce confusion about two war novels with similar titles, Heller increased his "catch" by four, strengthening the title in the process. (For some reason, possibly the repeating "t" sound, 22 sounds more absurd.)

Catch-22 appeared in 1961, the same year as *Mila-18*. More recently, though, with an ever-greater number of books bring printed, the earlier impulse of seeking originality or at least distinctiveness in book titles appears to have been abandoned in the mania to get out more books.

Even though it's now easy with the Internet to check the Library of Congress catalog and other websites to find titles that have already been used, authors and publishers seem inclined to recycle certain phrases, regardless of prior publication. Something that worked before might work again, so their thinking must go.

For instance, in 1996, Edward Klein's *All Too Human: The Love Story of Jack and Jackie Kennedy* came out. Three years later, former Clinton administration adviser George Stephanopoulos dissected the president he'd served in *All Too Human: A Political Education*. Both titles bring to mind Nietzsche's late-nineteenth-century treatise *Human, All Too Human*.

When Seymour Hersh's *The Dark Side of Camelot* appeared in 1997, I checked my study's shelf devoted to politicians and their private lives (an increasingly crowded section) and found a copy of Nelson Thompson's *The Dark Side of Camelot*, which the Playboy Press put out in 1976. Same subject, same title.

In a similar vein, Murray Sperber called his 1993 study of the early years of Notre Dame football *Shake Down the Thunder*. Two decades before, Wells Twombly's biography of former Notre Dame coach Frank Leahy was titled—you guessed it—*Shake Down the Thunder*. The Iranian hostage crisis of 1979 and 1980 triggered several books, including Barbara Henneger's *October Surprise* in 1989 and Gary Sick's *October Surprise* in 1991. But Bonnie MacDougal's recent thriller, *Out of Order*, is not to be confused with Thomas E. Patterson's *Out of Order*, a 1993 award-winning study of the media's coverage of political life.

Browsing in a library not long ago, I felt as if I were trapped in a batting cage—or a verbal echo chamber. I kept running into books with the word "Hardball" on the cover.

On the "Just Published" rack was the new edition of columnist and commentator Chris Matthews's analysis of contemporary politics, which sparked the high-hard-one approach to civic discourse he conducts nightly on the cable talkfest *Hardball*. Over in sports, there was a copy of *Hardball: The Education of a Baseball Commissioner*, by Bowie Kuhn, who redefined the word controversy during his stint as the game's czar. Nearby were two other *Hardball* books about the same sport: Doug Honig's, which appeared in 1985 (two years before Kuhn's memoir), and Dick Giebel's baseball journal that came out in 1993. In the section devoted to urban affairs, there was Daniel Coyle's *Hardball: A Season in the Projects*, about inner-city baseball in Chicago, which was also published in 1993.

Up in fiction, a wandering reader found English mystery writer Jimmy Sangster's 1988 novel *Hardball*, which goes with his series that includes *Snowball* and *Blackball*. Chicago author Barbara D'Amato launched her string of successful Cat Marsala mysteries with her version of *Hardball* in 1990. Since then D'Amato (and Marsala) have engaged audiences with *Hard Tack, Hard Luck, Hard Women, Hard Case, Hard Christmas, Hard Bargain,* and *Hard Evidence.*

Like John D. MacDonald's use of colors for his Travis McGee novels (*The Deep Blue Good-By* or *Free Fall in Crimson*), or Sue Grafton's alphabetical approach (*"A" Is for Alibi* to the most recent, *"O" Is for Outlaw*), or Harry Kemelman's reliance on days (*Tuesday the Rabbi Saw Red* or *Saturday the Rabbi Went Hungry*), D'Amato's titles have an internal consistency reflecting a certain originality. Despite the gimmicky quality to such a series, the titles remain distinctive and memorable, which should be an author's abiding objective.

"The Ancient Mariner would not have taken so well if it had been called 'The Old Sailor,'" British writer Samuel Butler once remarked of Samuel Coleridge's ballad *The Rime of the Ancient Mariner.* That's true, but somehow *The Old Man and the Sea* works perfectly as the title of the Ernest Hemingway novella. It's direct, definite, and descriptive, suggesting one person's confrontation with nature. The phrase, in fact, mirrors the stark simplicity of the book's prose.

Hemingway took titles seriously, commenting at one point: "I make a list of titles after I've finished the story or the book—sometimes as many as a hundred. Then I start eliminating them, sometimes all of them."

Coming up with a striking word or phrase for a title is serendipity squared. Although Hemingway was one author who waited until the end, other writers begin with a title, using it as the guiding star to a new book's last page. Sometimes a titular epiphany occurs midway into a project, helping to order and clarify the work in progress.

Walker Percy, who wrote such sensitively probing novels as *The Moviegoer, Love in the Ruins,* and *The Thanatos Syndrome,* believed, "A good title should be like a good metaphor: It should intrigue without being too baffling or obvious." Percy's own titles illustrate his point, as does his collection of essays, *Lost in the Cosmos: The Last Self-Help Book.* They arouse curiosity in a natural way. Percy also helped bring about the posthumous publication of John Kennedy Toole's aptly named comic *tour de force, A Confederacy of Dunces,* those words being a clever reworking of a line by Jonathan Swift.

Harper Lee took four words directly from the prose of her novel and artfully called what she'd written *To Kill a Mockingbird.* William Faulkner's *The*

Sound and the Fury, John Steinbeck's *The Grapes of Wrath,* and Graham Greene's *The Power and the Glory* are compelling phrases from other sources (a play, a hymn, and a prayer, respectively), but they effectively arouse a reader's interest—as well as make a point about the work they name.

I might be too much of a purist in this matter, but a book should be one of a kind, standing on its own as a unique creation of fiction or nonfiction. A copycat title is by no means the same as a copycat crime, yet it makes a reader wonder whether other words in the book are echoes of someone else's voice.

—*Chicago Tribune,* February 20, 2000

Process vs. Product

As a young writer (well before the infelicitous phrase "word processing" became popular), I'd annoyingly tell friends—or anyone who'd listen—about a current composition, quoting precisely from memory each word and punctuation mark.

The other day, however, when somebody asked about a new writing project, I stumbled around, trying to explain the general direction an essay was taking. After a few awkward attempts, I stopped, smiled, and offered to provide a copy of the finished product when it appeared.

Although personally unsettling (is this the dawn of a succession of so-called senior moments?), the recent exchange is instructive in its own way. At a certain point in a writer's life, the process of putting words together in a sequence, struggling for coherence, becomes what you do. That process itself—almost as much as satisfaction with completion of a work—turns into a curious and continuing obsession.

In part, I suppose, the more writing one does, the more the process develops into a routine, complete with the quirky, individualistic rituals of solitary work. But even the suggestion of a routine doesn't do justice to the compulsion to compose that, over time, becomes a writer's self-imposed yet strangely consoling servitude.

Not long ago, students in a class looked at me with more than customary disbelief as I said I no longer made any distinction when working on a book, an article for an academic journal, a magazine piece, a column for a news-paper, or a talk. Writing is writing, a continuing flow of words, with certain conventions applying for each form. There's nothing mystical about "authoring" a book, as some students imagined. The basics stay the same.

Even though experience helps develop a particular routine and, one hopes, a personal style or voice, the writing never—repeat never—gets easier. Each day starts with a blank page or screen, with myriad decisions awaiting.

To be sure, the more writing one does, the more predictable the process becomes. Days vary in terms of productivity, with the flow of words often turning into a trickle, but the years teach lessons or moves about openings, transitions, endings, and other aspects of word work.

Ernest Hemingway, who talked about writing with a romantic's reverence for a noble calling, once remarked, "We are all apprentices in a craft where no one ever becomes a master." Despite a host of physical problems and the demons of depression that haunted his final years, Hemingway kept writing—and not just to underwrite his globetrotting lifestyle and celebrated appetites. Indeed, A *Moveable Feast*, which occupied his final years and came out three years after he committed suicide in 1961, is an enduring memoir of Paris after World War I. American letters would be poorer without it.

When Hemingway's *True at First Light* appeared last summer to coincide with the one-hundredth anniversary of his birth in Oak Park, many reviewers questioned not only the literary merit but also the *raison d'être* of what the publisher called "a fictional memoir." Justifiable as this criticism is, there's also something humanly heroic about Hemingway's not abandoning his craft amid the turmoil of his own life, particularly the aftermath of the serious plane crash in 1954 that (among other injuries) fractured his skull and ruptured his liver, spleen, and one kidney.

In a similar way, Mark Twain spent the last years of his life coping with bankruptcy, a series of illnesses, and the grief of burying his wife and two daughters by making words his shield and sword. Of course, the pessimistic later writings (*The Man That Corrupted Hadleyburg, The Mysterious Stranger, What Is Man?* and several posthumous volumes of stories and fulminations) lack the roistering spirit and arresting interplay between childhood and adulthood of *Adventures of Huckleberry Finn* or *A Connecticut Yankee in King Arthur's Court*. But that's not the point.

Like Hemingway, Twain found necessary solace in his daily writing that was rewarding in itself. Yes, dark times yielded dark works. More significantly, though, his words became his refuge, with their strength sustaining.

For a Hemingway, a Twain, or a much less wounded and far less accomplished scribbler, the process itself, of being continuously involved in a project of whatever length or challenge, is critical. Someone once referred to life as a series of "can't helps"—you can't help doing something because you find it compelling or fulfilling.

Those who classify writing as a "can't help" realize that the completion of one project also serves as the prelude to the next one. Anthony Trollope, who gave the word "prolific" additional meaning in the nineteenth century with his fictional output, often began a new novel the same day he finished another one, never interrupting his daily regimen for composition.

After the publication of *Look Homeward, Angel* and *Of Time and the River*, Thomas Wolfe observed that "one writes a book not in order to remember it, but in order to forget it." This might sound paradoxical, even absurd— the ultimate expression that you can't go home again. But the more you write and draw on your memory in doing so (as Wolfe powerfully did in his massive novels), the more you tend to forget what you've written.

A few months ago, I kept feeling ashamed as I corrected the galleys of a new book. Someone else might just as well have composed certain sentences (and whole sections). The phrasing and how one point followed another surprised the reader, who earlier had been the writer.

A psychologist, undoubtedly, would identify a deteriorating short-term memory that comes with advancing years as the principal reason a person can't remember a recently completed composition. I, though, tend to see the matter somewhat differently.

In a mysterious yet natural way (after, say, the third or fourth book), the writing process itself becomes a consuming concern, a ritual of literary devotions. Tomorrow's words—and how they will dance together—are much more absorbing than yesterday's or others from the days before.

—*Chicago Tribune*, April 2, 2000

Between Books

A couple of centuries ago, the linguistically nimble British coined a term for it. Inspired by such words as "vicinity" and "extremity," they playfully wanted to denote an intermediate time or condition. Thus did "betweenity" enter the English usage. A cottage, to cite one example in the *Oxford English Dictionary*, languished "in a sad state of betweenity."

Whether sad or not, most authors know the meaning of a certain state of betweenness. After however long it takes—a year, two, more—a book appears, and while waiting for reviews to arrive, a low-grade anxiety begins. What's next? Where do I go from here? When's best to approach a publisher about a new manuscript?

Like finding oneself between jobs (if not quite a rock and a hard place), the period could most appropriately be described as being "between books." It's a time of competing feelings. The sense of freedom that you don't have the daily duty to a protracted project that assumes control of one's life jousts with nagging guilt that, even though you're writing with ritualistic regularity, it's not truly serious because it's not Authorship, with a capital "A."

Coming from America's heartland and sensitive to the rhythms of his region, Mark Twain repeatedly refers in his letters to what he calls his "fallow" periods. Though an imperfect judge of his prodigious output (for reasons unfathomable he considered the eminently forgettable *Personal Recollections of Joan of Arc* his most accomplished creation), Twain understood the natural processes of an author's life. In his reckoning and from his experience, one's subconscious could be a valuable ally not only between books but also during the composition of an extended, involved work.

With the intercession of inspiration (and some perspiration), fertile times follow fallow (on and off, *Adventures of Huckleberry Finn* took eight years to complete), and books eventually take shape to get published. Changing the metaphor but not the faith behind the idea, Twain observed: "When the tank runs dry you've only to leave it alone and it will fill up again in time."

As Twain well knew, being between books is by no means to be confused with writer's block. Many a wordsmith alternates between being a sprinter absorbed in relatively brief compositions and a marathoner committed to the, at times, seemingly interminable course of a book.

Scribbling short stuff of whatever kind can be a rewarding reprieve from the lonely vagaries of long-distance writing. Such projects take only days, not years, and there's a chance to work (and play) with several forms. Ideally, too, changing one's pace and finish line can serve a larger purpose, with results much more than five-finger exercises. Literary lightning can strike at any time.

Several years ago, very much between books, I was struggling to come to terms with the interplay between political culture and contemporary communications that defined so much of Ronald Reagan's two terms as president. As I was drafting a newspaper column about (of all subjects) Dan Quayle and humor, the phrase "statecraft and stagecraft" popped from my pencil without plan or fanfare.

Right then and there, those three words became the working title for a book with a specific theme and focus. A couple of years later, it appeared, complete with an explanatory subtitle: "American Political Life in the Age of Personality."

More recently—and to stress the serendipity of betweenity—I was idly looking out the window of a train in western Australia when the structure of a volume (bringing together previously published essays with new ones) magically presented itself. In that moment, an always-handy notebook and pen became more absorbing than the outback's never-uninteresting landscape. For better or worse, that effort (after more authorial anguish than the initial brainstorm might have anticipated) came out last year.

John Steinbeck probably underestimated the situation when he remarked that "book writing makes horse racing seem like a solid, stable business." You never know what book might be around the corner, nor how the finished product will compare to the original concept. As the flush of excitement over a new work subsides, day (or night) labor on it becomes something of a routine, with the last few months a frantic and curious mixture of relief and worry.

Part of the worry (absurd as it might sound) is that the author's unexpected demise, despite robust health, could prevent the book's publication—and that just can't happen. Instructions about extra copies of the manuscript or computer files solemnly become entrusted to others.

Yet, to be sure, arriving at "The End" of the process means it's only a matter of time before the feeling of being between books sets in. And the cycle starts again.

In the essay "Why I Write," George Orwell, who intrepidly exhibited mastery of the English language in forms long and short, puts matters in perspective:

"All writers are vain, selfish and lazy, and at the very bottom of their motives there lies a mystery. Writing a book is a horrible, exhausting struggle, like a long bout of some painful illness. One would never undertake such a thing if one were not driven on by some demon whom one can neither resist nor understand."

For many writers, the arrival of Orwell's demon follows an unannounced visit from a most-welcome muse. The real mystery of book writing lies in that strange mating dance between muse and demon, which often starts between books, when an author is wondering about the next adventure with words.

—*Chicago Tribune*, August 12, 2001

Reading Fellow Travelers

Call me, if you wish, a voyeur. For as long as I can remember, I've engaged in the bookworm's version of a busman's holiday. Wandering hither and yon, I always make a point of interrupting my own reading for furtive perusal of whatever's occupying the eyeballs of fellow travelers and those around me.

Some people, I suspect, might judge this nomadic avocation akin to an invasion of privacy. Yet in entering a plea of *nolo contendere*, I'd argue that this experiment in participation and observation provides not only guilty pleasures of a venial sort but also larger lessons about a country's culture.

On a recent trip to Paris, for instance, the Metro proved to be a moveable feast for a reader-watcher. Besides the predictable riffling through newspapers and the ever-popular *policiers* (or detective novels), I saw three people absorbed in French translations of Isaac Asimov's science fiction, one sitting back with a volume of Lorca's poems, and another oblivious to all as he read Kierkegaard's *Le Journal du Seducteur* (*Diary of a Seducer*).

It's chancy to generalize, but those rides and rubbernecking in cafes near Left Bank bookshops (with folks reading, among other writers, Milan Kundera, Baudelaire, even Tocqueville) reflected the opposite of a bestseller mentality. Individuals were following singular concerns with refreshing seriousness and, shall we say, Old World sophistication.

Here at home, a wanderer tends to see consumers of current events poring over newspapers or magazines; business-minded executives of both sexes mastering work-related publications or yet another of those half-horse-sense, half-horse-manure guides to leadership; students wielding yellow markers in their textbooks; men and women keeping up with the latest John Grisham, Danielle Steel, Stephen King, or Mary Higgins Clark; and (increasingly) souls seeking spiritual or inspirational sustenance from the printed page. Incongruously, perhaps, you rarely discover travelers engrossed in first-rate travel writing by, say, Jonathan Raban, Paul Theroux, or Bill Bryson.

In my unscientific study, popular fiction seems our most popular choice. As flight delays become *de rigueur* in American travel, the longer the book often means the longer the flyer's fuse. A popular author's potboiler can help a reader escape the boiling point of tedium to find a world of adventure, romance or at least bearable diversion.

Interestingly, for all the talk about electronic books and the hand-held gizmos for reading them that store up to a dozen titles, you see relatively few travelers using them. I did spy a woman at Chicago's O'Hare International Airport with one the other day, but during an eternity of waiting there, it's possible to witness almost anything.

A long O'Hare layover can become an intellectual adventure in itself. An academic colleague—with powers of concentration I envy and an absent-mindedness I don't—became so engrossed in Paul Johnson's *Modern Times* that his much-delayed flight ended up departing without him. By the time he got home (to a none-too-happy wife, he reported), most of the book's eight hundred pages were marked with comments and quarrels.

Reading of such seriousness might be foreign to most roaming, but I know several people who relish extended trips by themselves, primarily for the sake of catching up on new books and other publications. Emerson might have famously viewed nineteenth-century travel as "a fool's paradise," but today it serves as a reader's refuge, removed from quotidian demands and distractions.

Which is one reason my until-now-secret hobby holds a curious fascination. Taking a crowded subway in Washington a few months ago, I stood next to a young man who was holding a book with one hand and a safety pole with the other. His sly, mischievous, half smile immediately piqued my interest. An unobtrusive step for a closer look at the object of his attention revealed all: Vladimir Nabokov's *Lolita*.

A few weeks later, during a sojourn in Dublin, I went to the taxi rank at St. Stephen's Green to catch a cab. The driver in position to take the next fare didn't look up until I tapped on his window, and even then he seemed somewhat perturbed. He was reading a book, with several others spread out on the seat next to him.

As I happily switched from watcher to listener, my ride to meetings at University College Dublin became a traffic-snarled tutorial in Irish literature, with passing references to British and American authors. From this uncommon common reader ("I'd say I've got seven or eight thousand books at home") I learned much, including that Seamus Heaney's new collection of poetry, *Electric Light*, was already a top seller throughout the country and that Heaney, a Nobel laureate in literature, is so well-known in his native Ireland it's difficult for him to go anywhere without attracting an adoring crowd.

En route, he also spoke passionately about Joyce, Yeats, Flann O'Brien, and John McGahern—not to mention Flannery O'Connor and William Faulkner, his favorite American writers. I've never regretted the end of a cab ride until that one.

Leaving Dublin on a flight to London, I glanced across the aisle and two unoccupied seats to check what a stoutish, ample-chinned woman in the afternoon of her years was reading. It was a magazine article whose title posed an age-old question: "Do You Need Some Sexual Energy?" She didn't turn the page for a long time.

Reading readers as they travel might make me an economy-class Peeping Tom in need of counseling, a support group, or both. Denial notwithstanding, I see the practice as somewhat less risky—and even more rewarding—than the one advocated by Oscar Wilde. "I never travel without my diary," the scandalous wit once wrote. "One should always have something sensational to read in the train."

—*Chicago Tribune*, August 26, 2001

The Gift of New Life

Not long ago, after I tried explaining what I had been hoping to do in a little book assigned for discussion, a student lingered while others headed for the door. Curious about the vagaries and mysteries of composition, she wanted to know what part of the writing process I found most rewarding and satisfying.

Is it—to paraphrase her probing, double-barreled question—the fitting together, bricklayer fashion, of words that somehow hold together without unduly offending a reader's eye (or ear), or the eventual appearance, with fanfare or not, of a finished work following a lengthy period of gestation?

Taken somewhat aback and remarking that the inquiry was similar to forcing a parent to pick a favorite child, I responded in (I fear) typical academic fashion by rejecting either alternative. In my experience—and in all truthfulness—I favor what you might call a written effort's reincarnation, its second, even third life beyond the time it came into being or first appeared.

I could tell from her quizzical expression that she was now taken aback, so I elaborated on what I meant.

Usually out of the blue—via letter, call or, increasingly, e-mail—you learn that an article or book will be reprinted or translated. Someone somewhere finds enough merit in what you've composed to grant it another existence that was neither planned nor anticipated.

Although a fair share of readers might consider the literary reincarnation we're talking about as the lazy, anguish-free route to publication, I view the matter somewhat differently. More than a heartening review or complimentary letter, a request for reprinting or translation is the formal acceptance of a piece of work that another word-oriented worthy acknowledges and wants to distribute in a new format.

Besides its being a stamp of some kind of approval, there are other, more personal reasons for taking delight in this after-the-presses-roll notice. Yes, additional money arrives, albeit in my league usually in munificent sums that will just about cover the cost of the writing pads on which I scribble.

More helpfully, a request might appear when a work in progress shows little progress after much work. To know that an earlier effort will have another life can reassure a fretful soul, longing to hear an encouraging word.

In some cases, too, there's the small yet exhilarating satisfaction that an all-but-forgotten composition from years ago was remembered and tucked away for use today. It somehow makes the solitary busyness of stringing words together a little less momentary—and lonely.

In *Red*, an engrossing biography of the late sportswriter and artful stylist Red Smith, Ira Berkow points out another virtue of post-publication publication. He reports how "Smith tried to establish his credentials" with five new and not-altogether-accepting stepchildren when he remarried after his first wife died. Among other stratagems to suggest he was more than a garden-variety ink-stained wretch, he (according to Berkow) made use of "a college textbook, A *Quarto of Modern Literature,* which contained a piece that he had written on Joe Louis. It was the only newspaper article in the book, and it was between an essay by Winston Churchill and a poem by Dylan Thomas. Red left the book on the kitchen table, with the page open to his place."

In other words (or so Smith hoped to show), he was, indeed, somebody, with talents as remarkable in their way as those of the athletes he distinctively described.

As enjoyable and ego enhancing as this type of reincarnation might be, granting someone permission to use your work is something of a shot in the dark. How your words will appear is generally a mystery, so you wait like anybody else to see the new version.

As Smith knew, the company you keep in a collection can do wonders for the spirit. There's also an exotic enchantment to beholding translations of a book or article in unfamiliar languages and alphabets.

Such romance, however, does occasionally collide with reality, deflating one's chest and making matters cruelly laughable. A little over a year ago, e-mail brought a we've-tried-to-reach-you-before message inquiring about reprint rights to a Sunday newspaper feature that had appeared several months earlier. A textbook was going to press forthwith, and a "yes" or "no" was necessary immediately.

Recalling that some paragraphs had been trimmed in the original copy to make way for what the humble writer judged to be an excessively large picture, I said I'd be delighted to provide the unexpurgated text for the book in question. It was too late to consider any additions, the publisher's agent reported. Somewhat downcast but still pleased, I agreed to their terms.

Well, when the volume arrived, I eagerly searched for one particular contribution, which I even more quickly discovered failed to carry a byline. Following the last word of the article was a minuscule number 1 as the only footnote. Additional riffling through the book took me to page 649—472 pages later—and a credit line buried amid bifocal-challenging type. So much for any fleeting feeling about pride of authorship.

Chancy as the reprint experience can be, it still to my mind trumps the alternative of singular exposure, because it always widens the circle of potential readers. Surprisingly, however, this immodest opinion finds resistance in certain quarters. Three decades before he died, British poet A. E. Housman implored his publisher, "You must not treat my immortal works as quarries to be used at will by the various hacks whom you employ to compile anthologies."

No weaver of words, especially a respected poet, wants "hacks" plundering a corpus of work. But authentic immortality of the literary sort comes, in part, from repeated publication over time. To restrict the possibility limits future appraisal and the prospect of rediscovery by subsequent generations.

A Housman contemporary, critic and book-minded journalist James Agate, had a more realistic view about the value of staying in print. In one of the most melancholic diary entries I've ever encountered, Agate wrote, "Today I am a lamppost against which no anthologist lifts his leg."

Possibly offensive yet positively memorable, that single sentence expresses the true writer's aching fear of being forgotten and the desperate yearning to keep one's words alive.

—*Chicago Tribune*, March 3, 2002

The Reviewing Stand

In the extended family of literary journalism, book reviewing often struggles to avoid being considered a shirttail relation of dubious parentage. Neither full-dress, argument-buttoned-down essay nor searching, multivoice article, a review begins its existence with something of an inferiority complex. Its relatively few words appear in a recyclable newspaper or magazine—and increasingly today on the even more evanescent Internet—solely because someone else has written thousands more words for safekeeping between cloth covers.

To a certain extent, every review creates a David versus Goliath encounter. This doesn't—or shouldn't—mean the reviewer is in a perpetual contest for the last word, or that the goal of a journalistic critique is to expedite a book's sentence to the remainder pile, or, worse, pulping factory. But a review does come to the public overshadowed by its subject—an object of greater size and considerably more weight.

In biological terms, you might even say a review has a certain parasitic quality, as it lives off something else. Without a book, there'd be no review.

More revealing than metaphors in sizing up reviewing as a genre are the views of literary artists about those rendering critical judgments. Early in the nineteenth century, with book publishing and periodicals with reaction expanding, English poet Samuel Taylor Coleridge fired a first volley in what has become a continuing verbal skirmish: "Reviewers are usually people who would have been poets, historians, biographers, &c., if they could; they have tried their talents at one or at the other, and have failed; therefore they turn critics."

More colorfully, Irish writer and *enfant terrible* Brendan Behan noted that reviewers "are like eunuchs in a harem: they know how it's done, they've seen it done every day, but they're unable to do it themselves."

Put-downs, it seems, are *de rigueur* in describing those assigned to appraise another's work. The late Alfred Kazin, one of America's most respected commentators on literature during the last half of the twentieth century, begins his memoir, *Writing Was Everything*, by quoting Goethe's growl: "Kill the dog, he's a reviewer!" Kazin, himself the producer of countless reviews, goes on to say, "The many composers, artists, and writers who like me have suffered and never forgotten a single line in a bad review still cheer Goethe on."

It's easier nowadays for reviewers to shrug off vituperative descriptions of their work for a simple reason. With the independent, freelance public intellectual and person of letters vanishing-to-extinct as a literary species, most women and men turning out reviews today have separate, defining identities and other sources of income. For an academic, novelist, poet, journalist, whatever, a review becomes piecework, an assignment to take on amid other word-related responsibilities.

Gone are the days when a Van Wyck Brooks, Malcolm Cowley, or Edmund Wilson could make their way as writers by primarily rendering judgments on books as they appeared. In Wilson's case (and to a lesser extent with the others), he periodically collected his reviews in popular books of his own, including *The Shores of Light, Classics and Commercials*, and *The Bit Between My Teeth*.

In her recent volume of essays, *Sight-Readings*, Elizabeth Hardwick refers to Wilson as "one of our country's supreme men of letters," an opinion still widely shared thirty years after his death in 1972. Yet even Wilson wasn't immune to dismissal.

From undergraduate days in the 1960s and a fondly remembered class on literary satire, I've kept paperback copies of several novels by Evelyn Waugh: *Scoop, Vile Bodies*, and *Put Out More Flags* (among others). The back cover of each features one phrase by Wilson about Waugh: "The only first-rate comic genius that has appeared in English since Bernard Shaw."

The other day, while browsing in a posthumously published edition of Waugh's diaries, I ran across this brief but eye-opening entry from 1945, a few months after Wilson wrote his much-quoted line: "chucked appointment to show London to insignificant Yank named Edmund Wilson, critic."

A hundred or so pages later, another notation reveals Waugh's broader view of the reviewing trade: "Reading the papers, and especially the literary reviews, is like sitting in a railroad carriage and hearing a fellow-passenger pointing out to a companion passing objects of interest and getting them all wrong."

Waugh, an ironist's ironist and congenital naysayer, frequently contributed to British newspapers, including his share of reviews. One's left to wonder whether his diaries served as his personal confessional, a place to tell the truth, or whether they were the private repository of cleverly snide remarks of a piece with his other prose—or whether they were both.

Reviews by their nature are ephemeral, with only a handful of writers having the literary clout and cachet to gather such work in subsequent books. In recent years, John Updike, Thomas Mallon, and Martin Amis have come out with collections featuring their reviews, but they are exceptions principally because they are exceptional stylists.

Most reviews survive, if at all, as unrecognizable shadows of themselves in the form of individual, blurblike lines in book ads or as endorsing statements on paperback editions. Much like movie promoters with their block-buster-minded advertising featuring crowd-attracting phrases, publishers package and present praise with scrupulous disregard for nuance and context. Only the most positive words and phrases receive a second life, and they often appear quite differently from their original presentation.

Take, for instance, Wilson's line about Waugh's following in Shaw's footsteps. Those words came at the end of a lengthy disquisition on Waugh's early fiction and how those novels compare to F. Scott Fitzgerald's *The Great Gatsby* and Ernest Hemingway's *The Sun Also Rises*. Here's Wilson's complete statement, with "they" referring to Waugh's novels:

"They are not so poetic; they are perhaps less intense; they belong to a more classical tradition. But I think that they are likely to last and that Waugh, in fact, is likely to figure as the only first-rate comic genius that has appeared in English since Bernard Shaw."

The hedging that comes from the repetition of "likely" surely makes the publisher's rendering on all those paperbacks more of a seal of approval than Wilson intended.

A few years ago, while visiting a bookstore to survey new titles, I was surprised to discover my own name decorating the front cover of the paperback version of *All's Fair*, the dual memoir by Mary Matalin and James Carville about their work for opposing candidates during the 1992 presidential race and how they, subsequently, got married.

Yes, it is true I wrote the words: "The ultimate insider tale . . . takes the reader inside a presidential campaign as no other book has . . . engrossing." But those words are wrenched from three separate sentences in three different paragraphs in a twenty-one-paragraph review.

The remark about taking a reader inside a campaign precedes the review's last sentence: "From a citizen's perspective, the lessons learned are well worth knowing—and worrying about." The word "engrossing" comes from a phrase in the first paragraph, calling the account "simultaneously engrossing and unsettling." The review's unifying theme was that the book should be read as a cautionary tale about questionable practices of contemporary politics. But, I guess, "all's fair" in politics and publishing.

Truth be told, words from reviews also live on at the other extreme from putatively high praise. Some sharply pointed statements of dismissal are so delectably memorable they find their way into compilations of quotations, like James Charlton's *Fighting Words* and Bob Perlongo's engaging new volume, *The Write Book*.

In the late 1920s and early 1930s, giftedly acerbic Dorothy Parker conducted the "Constant Reader" column for the *New Yorker*. Reacting to A. A. Milne's *The House at Pooh Corner*, she confessed: "Tonstant Weader fwowed up." About a multivolume (and self-indulgent) autobiography by Margot Asquith, she wrote: "The affair between Margot Asquith and Margot Asquith will live as one of the prettiest love stories in all literature." A justly forgotten work of fiction was dispatched thusly: "This is not a novel to be tossed aside lightly. It should be thrown with great force."

Such zingers deserve perpetuity. Others that aren't nearly so inspired linger exclusively in the mind of the person whose book has been publicly mugged. Here Kazin's earlier perception gains weighty pertinence. No author on the receiving end of what he or she judges an unjust assessment ever forgets the abusive treatment of a miscreant who has savaged a literary offspring.

To be sure, an author can learn from legitimate criticism, and occasionally a reviewer hears from a writer expressing gratitude for suggesting points to pursue in the future. Just as importantly, a thoughtful and thorough review can help an author see the necessity of approaching reviewing assignments of one's own in a fair, open-minded manner.

"Writing even a bad book is hard work," novelist Richard Ford once remarked. Responsible reviewers realize this, striving to maintain a balanced view of a book's strengths and weaknesses for an overall judgment.

While serving time in graduate school (and plotting how to combine a life of teaching and writing), I picked up a collection of smartly written reviews by Anthony Burgess, the English author best known for his novel *A Clockwork Orange*. His title, *Urgent Copy*, struck me then (and now) as a fitting journalistic description of reviewing: timely reportage and analysis concerning books of consequence as they are coming into the world.

In the years before e-mail—and in secret homage to Burgess—I boldly printed URGENT COPY across the top of any review before faxing it off to a newspaper or magazine. My youthful enthusiasm about literary commentary notwithstanding, books do serve as the cornerstones of culture. Reviewing not only acquaints readers with books that are testaments of our time but also contributes to the continuing conversation within the republic of letters.

—*Chicago Tribune*, August 4, 2002

HEADNOTE

I knew next to nothing about Ireland or Irish literature before being invited to teach about America at University College Dublin in 2000. Since living there then, I've returned once or twice a year, reveling in the constant interplay among literature, history, politics, and religion that seems indigenous to that island. I make no claim to expertise, but studying certain aspects of Irish literary life has become a welcome hobby—something of a busman's holiday—and one path to more general historical and sociopolitical understanding.

The following essay is a prosy celebration of Dublin, a city with pride of its wordsmiths you don't find anywhere else. One frequently heard precept of that city's pub wisdom is the wisecrack: "Here a writer is no more than a failed talker." V. S. Pritchett, the British critic and writer, identified in George Bernard Shaw's massive output what he called "an Irish addiction to words," a cultural trait unavoidable in Dublin and throughout the island.

The next piece is more reportorial, examining the controversy Frank McCourt's globally successful memoir, *Angela's Ashes*, ignited in the city of his youth, Limerick. Since the article appeared, I've met and gotten to know the author. During a post-lecture discussion at Notre Dame in 2003, McCourt was quizzed about the accuracy of his personal writing and the possibility of embellishment. He responded: "Well, there are facts in there, but then you have to fill in spaces between. Somebody asked me in San Francisco one night, why didn't you write a novel? Nobody would believe it, if I wrote a novel about what it was like growing up in Limerick and what it was like coming to New York. The main story or structure is there, but then you have to paint and put on wallpaper and things like that."

Debating details of what someone remembers and renders might generate heat, but what endures is the light of vivid and inspired writing, which *Angela's Ashes* certainly features.

Writers and Dublin Town

DUBLIN, Ireland—With a precision of emotion that comes from a scarred memory, James Joyce describes the stifling surroundings that stunt the literary growth of his autobiographical protagonist in A *Portrait of the Artist as a Young Man*. At one point Joyce writes of Stephen: "His sensitive nature was still smarting under the lashes of an undivined and squalid way of life. His soul was still disquieted and cast down by the dull phenomenon of Dublin."

Joyce himself escaped "the dull phenomenon of Dublin" by living most of his nearly fifty-nine years as an exile in Paris and elsewhere in Europe. He never returned to Ireland after 1912 (when he was thirty), even though all his major works—*Dubliners* (1914), *Portrait of the Artist* (1916), *Ulysses* (1922), and *Finnegans Wake* (1939)—are set in Dublin and examine every facet of Irish life.

Joyce was not alone in leaving his native, green grounds to pursue the literary muse. Oscar Wilde and George Bernard Shaw before him as well as Samuel Beckett and Edna O'Brien later found life abroad more conducive to developing their writing. Beckett, who, like Shaw, won a Nobel Prize for literature, spoke not only for himself when he complained about Dublin's "oppressive Catholic atmosphere" as a principal stricture on freedom of expression and rendering warts-and-all reality.

But times change. Especially in recent years, as Ireland has become more secular, prosperous, and artistically accepting, there's been a concerted effort to celebrate the talents of writers who left home and gained international recognition. In Dublin, it's impossible to wander very far without discovering a statue, plaque, or entire building honoring the achievements of a literary expatriate.

This attitude that all is forgiven is also reflected in Dublin's numerous bookshops, where volumes by Joyce, Wilde, Shaw, and Beckett occupy as much shelf space as that devoted to noted contemporary Irish poets and novelists, such as Seamus Heaney, Roddy Doyle, Eavan Boland, Seamus Deane, and John Banville—not to mention Maeve Binchy.

Most remarkable (and unavoidable), Dublin's homage to Joyce is replete with Joycean irony, given that *Ulysses* takes place in (to quote the author) "the city of failure, of rancour and of unhappiness." His bust in St. Stephen's Green looks pensively toward Newman House of University College Dublin, where he studied. A life-size statue, complete with hat, glasses, and walking stick, stands just off O'Connell Street in the city's busiest downtown area, attracting a constant stream of onlookers and picturetakers.

Not far from the statue is the James Joyce Centre, a stately Georgian house that organizes exhibits, lectures, reading groups, and other activities about Joyce and his work. Since opening in 1996, the Centre has made the celebration of Bloomsday—June 16, 1904, the day *Ulysses* takes place—a weeklong festival of dramatic readings, tours, talks, and social occasions. The centenary of Bloomsday in 2004 promises to be almost as active as Joyce's imagination, with planning already afoot.

Just outside Dublin in Sandycove, the James Joyce Tower is not only a museum with manuscripts, first editions, and the writer's memorabilia. It is also the defense tower built by the British in 1804 where Joyce briefly lived and set the vivid opening scene of *Ulysses*. From its gun platform on top, he could survey all of Dublin, the city he physically left yet kept returning to in his mind and work.

Although some of Joyce's relatives remember being told in the 1940s and 1950s not to reveal their kinship with the author because (among other things) his religious irreverence and open treatment of sex angered many Irish, it's now possible to trace the scene changes of *Ulysses* by following fourteen brass pavement markers placed around the city. At 52 Clanbrassil Street in what used to be Dublin's Jewish quarter, one even finds a wall plaque to honor the fictional birthplace of Joyce's fictional character Leopold Bloom—"Citizen, Husband, Father, Wanderer, Reincarnation of Ulysses."

Much of the transformation of Dublin into a citywide literary theme park has taken place since 1990. In that time, besides the Joycean jubilance that extends to T-shirts, mugs, and other usual tourist merchandise, the house where George Bernard Shaw was born and spent the first decade of his ninety-four-year life has been carefully restored and opened to the public. Three years ago, a reclining statue of a dandified Oscar Wilde was dedicated at Merrion Square. The lifelike, full-color rendering of the increasingly popular dramatist, poet, and novelist looks out on pillars that reproduce some of his epigrams as well as the home across the street where his savage wit came into the world.

Yet honoring individual authors who became exiles is just one dimension to celebrating literary life in Ireland's capital city. The Dublin Writers Museum, which opened in 1991, provides context and background for understanding why myriad forms of composition have flourished in this one locale since Jonathan Swift set his satiric pen to paper in the eighteenth century. Drawing some fifty thousand visitors a year, the museum helps explain why a "reverence for words" has been an Irish trait for hundreds of years.

Ironically, as one informational panel at the museum points out, many of the writers most revered in Dublin "practiced their art in a language not indigenous to this country." Wilde, Shaw, Joyce, and their successors put their own stamps of originality on the English language, doing little or nothing with native Irish.

"It has been claimed that the greatest weapon the English ever gave to the Irish was their own language," a museum sign wryly notes, adding that "the language of the invader fueled the literature of the subversive" until the 1921 independence from Great Britain (for all but six northern counties) and the creation of the Irish Free State.

That literature, of course, was often composed by exiles abroad. But their work (in another ironic twist), along with the fiction, poetry and plays by those who never left what Shaw referred to as "John Bull's Other Island," greatly contributed to a distinct national identity. Appropriately, critic Declan Kiberd calls his illuminating study of Irish literature (from Wilde to the present) *Inventing Ireland*.

W. B. Yeats, the first of four Dublin natives or residents to win the Nobel Prize for literature in the twentieth century, once remarked, "If you want to know Ireland, body and soul, you must read its poems and stories." Dublin's celebration of writers doesn't only take someone closer to the "body and soul" of Ireland but also to enduring literary art.

—*Chicago Tribune*, August 13, 2000

Two Tales of One City

LIMERICK, Ireland—Although commentators on Frank McCourt's *Angela's Ashes* point out the memoir's Dickensian qualities of a hard-knocks youth struggling to cope with abject poverty through pluck and artful dodging, here in Limerick—McCourt's childhood home—a visitor hears two tales of one city.

For some residents of Ireland's third largest city, McCourt deserves the acclaim that comes from selling over four million copies and winning prestigious awards, like a Pulitzer Prize. For others, the former schoolteacher turned author exaggerates incidents from his experience to paint an overly bleak picture of Limerick life during the 1930s and 1940s.

As with many subjects up for debate in Ireland today, the argument over *Angela's Ashes* reflects a debate over what constitutes history and what qualifies as truth.

McCourt's success earned for him an honorary doctorate from the University of Limerick and a stint there as writer in residence. Since 1997, a daily walking tour of places figuring in *Angela's Ashes* has become popular. Brochures bill the two-hour excursion as a chance to see locations from "the Pulitzer Prize winning book by Dr. Frank McCourt." That phrase, in bold capital letters, reflects both American validation, important in Ireland, and Limerick's own recognition of McCourt's accomplishment.

John Logan, who's taught Irish history in Limerick since 1974, speaks for many when he praises McCourt's storytelling ability and the book's unwillingness to sentimentalize the past. "This is one man's experience, and to me there's nothing outlandish about it," says Logan, a senior lecturer at the University of Limerick.

"His detailing of the big issues—housing, health, the sociology of education, the influence of the clergy, the all-powerful bourgeoisie—all of that is very accurate."

Calling *Angela's Ashes* "a book about survival," Logan remarks, "I'm intensely proud of Limerick, and I was certainly not offended by it. I was moved by it. In the end, the criterion is honesty. Do I think McCourt's been honest? Yes."

Edward Horgan, twenty-year veteran of the Irish military who's lived in Limerick over a decade, remembers his own childhood in Tralee and identifies with much of McCourt's experience. He, however, emphasizes "the additional deprivation inflicted on the McCourt family by the father's alcoholism. Many of McCourt's contemporaries who lived in similar housing conditions fared much better because their fathers provided better support and parenting than Malachy McCourt did for his family."

Horgan, who has more relatives in Boston than in Ireland, explains that the growth of the University of Limerick has been a magnet for economic development in recent years, with one consequence being the bulldozing and rebuilding of slum areas described in *Angela's Ashes*.

Indeed, Limerick residents on either side of the controversy report with pride that producers of the recently released movie version went to Cork and Dublin to film scenes of poverty and lane life. Today's Limerick reflects the prosperity and dynamism of the so-called Celtic Tiger, complete with its expanding high-tech industry. The other day, for instance, Dell Computer announced the addition of 600 more employees to a staff of 4,580 already working at three Limerick facilities.

Some natives of this River Shannon city see the current boom time as a key reason people criticize *Angela's Ashes*. McCourt is dredging up a past they'd now prefer to avoid—or even forget. Topics such as the Irish Civil War and a family's personal problems or bygone political allegiances don't deserve public airing from their perspective. There are more important matters at hand.

McCourt's most vocal critic here is Gerard Hannan. As unrelenting as the rain in *Angela's Ashes*, Hannan is a local radio talk-show host and author obsessed with McCourt's rendering of the past. To date he's written two books challenging McCourt's recollections, and he's documented some 125 putative mistakes or inconsistencies in *Angela's Ashes*.

Hannan, who also owns a downtown bookstore featuring tables stacked with autographed copies of his own literary efforts, is a Limerick booster. As he says in *Ashes*, ". . . there are two sides to every story. Indeed there was dire poverty and hardship on the lanes of Limerick and that is a simple fact. However, hundreds of Limerick people endured and survived the poverty to live happy lives."

Hannan's most recent book, *'Tis in Me Ass* (a response to McCourt's current bestseller, *'Tis*) asks the question, "What became of the people who didn't run off to America but instead stayed at home to help build a city?" McCourt's ambition to return to America, the country of his birth, plays a role in the continuing controversy. As strong as the relationship between the U.S. and Ireland is, McCourt's memoir justifies emigration from the Emerald Isle, rankling some people here.

Hannan uses his radio program to re-ignite the smoldering debate. In January, as the film of *Angela's Ashes* opened here, he welcomed to the airwaves Limerick-born stage and screen actor Richard Harris, who proceeded to call McCourt "probably the ugliest and most bitter man I have ever met in my entire life."

Harris elaborated on his outrage in the *Sunday Times* of London, arguing that McCourt's "anger and his opportunism blinded him into distortion, ignoring a nation in resuscitation. Instead, he sought a theme of sickening self-pity, relying on fabrication and lies, never believing that one day he would be challenged."

What you hear from longtime Limerick residents critical of McCourt, including shopkeepers and taxi drivers, is the somewhat contradictory charge that he remembered too well (by naming real names and places) *and* that he falsely remembered—or fabricated—incidents (by exaggerating what actually happened). Some go so far as to charge McCourt with "Paddywhackery," a reliance on stage-Irish stereotypes to appeal to an American audience.

To varying degrees, however, everyone agrees the portrayal of McCourt's mother is a problem. While Logan calls the rendering "one-dimensional," Harris boils: "Limerick is alive and well and can defend itself; Angela isn't and can't. If you can attack your mother's morals by the insinuation of whore-dom—as McCourt did in his book—a woman whose only crime was to feed and house her children, then I suppose anybody, any place or anything is vulnerable."

It is, indeed, curious that McCourt's alcohol-loving, work-hating father is treated with cushioning nuance. Seeing three distinct people in his father, including the drunken one "who does the bad thing," McCourt writes, "I feel sad over the bad thing but I can't back away from him because the one in the morning is my real father and if I were in America I could say, I love you, Dad, the way they do in the films, but you can't say that in Limerick for fear you might be laughed at. You're allowed to say you love God and babies and horses that win but anything else is a softness in the head."

No such poignant passages appear about McCourt's mother, puzzling many here, especially those who knew Angela before she emigrated to the U.S. a decade after her son. She died in 1981.

Despite the controversy, Irish readers are deciding for themselves what to think of McCourt. In Limerick recently, the checkout person at the downtown library offered that ten people remained on a waiting list for *Angela's Ashes* and sixty for *'Tis*. Few inquire about Hannan's responses, she said. The Dublin Public Library ranked *Angela's Ashes* first and *'Tis* second as most-borrowed nonfiction books of 1999.

Eason, Ireland's leading distributor of books and magazines, reported that *Angela's Ashes* was its best-selling title last year. Interestingly, the company classified the book as "Irish/fiction."

Nonfictional or fictional, historically truthful or creatively contrived, the debate in Limerick over *Angela's Ashes* shows the acuity behind American writer John Barth's conclusion about any autobiographical account—"The story of your life is not your life. It is your story."

—*Boston Sunday Globe*, March 5, 2000

PART III

Matters Personal

Some of the preceding essays could quite legitimately appear in this section with its first-person emphasis. But it makes more sense, I think, to group literary pursuits together in their own sequence. Whether apparent or not, the main writing and bookish points are intended to offer a broader view of the writing craft, while the principal focus in the pieces to follow revolves around one individual, specific experiences, and personal responses. If you judge I'm splitting hairs, that's your opinion, and you might be right.

Most of these articles came into being after something—or a related series of actions or thoughts—occurred. In the preface to Lyrical Ballads, *Wordsworth famously remarks that "poetry is the spontaneous overflow of powerful feelings," deriving from "emotion recollected in tranquility." It would be both unseemly and fraudulent to make any comparisons, but in these efforts I try, however futilely, to capture experience and to reflect on its meaning in the manner and words a prose-bound scribbler thought appropriate for the occasion. I'm still waiting for tranquility.*

These pieces, which are arranged chronologically, come in all sizes: short, medium, and long. In some cases, humor, or at least an attempt at playfulness, seemed fitting for the circumstances. Laughter isn't always the best medicine, but self-directed deprecation can help erect the necessary walls to keep out any suggestion of self-indulgence. Joking aside, these articles provide some snapshots, in words, of a life much too tame ever to merit a full-fledged memoir.

The End of the Wrigley Connection

A Russian newspaper recently announced that the Soviet Union is going into the gum business. *Zhevatelnaya ryezinka*—literally, "chewing rubber"—is now on sale in Estonia, and a gum factory will open in Moscow next year.

For most Americans, I suppose, the news carries little meaning. It produces at most a smirky nod, acknowledging that even our questionable habits are exportable.

For others, however, especially those of us with a venal streak, the announcement possesses somewhat greater significance. It signals an end, once and for all, to the Wrigley connection.

To explain the inner workings of the Wrigley connection, one needs to be confessional.

Before I left on a visit to the Soviet Union a few years ago, a friend just back from a tour of Eastern Europe instructed me to take plenty of chewing gum and ballpoint pens as gifts for the Russians I would be meeting. He said these items were not available there, and that they served as small but meaningful favors. At his advice and in the spirit of being a gracious tourist, twenty-five packs of gum and around seventy cheap pens were tucked in an extra pair of shoes when I landed at the Moscow airport late one Sunday evening.

In retrospect I guess it was the gold sportcoat I was wearing Monday that tipped people off I wasn't a Soviet native. Wherever I seemed to walk, young, smiling men approached me and acted uncommonly solicitous about my health and welfare. Few knew more than a word or two of English—"Hello. How are you?"—so I did little more than smile a "fine" and keep walking.

Around noon, however, right in the middle of Red Square, a youth blocked my path and asked in rather fluent English if I was enjoying my sight-seeing. We struck up a conversation, and this led to the real reason for the encounter: How much did I want for the sunglasses I was wearing? I told him it was the only pair I had, and I didn't want to part with them.

He accepted this response, but, as they say, was not to be denied some kind of purchase. "You're chewing gum. I give you five rubles for a pack of gum."

Since five rubles are more than five dollars in the rate of exchange, I thought I had misunderstood what he said. Surely, I said to him, you mean five kopecks, roughly a nickel.

He shook his head. The rubles were produced; the conscience was tested. I looked around to see if anyone was watching—black marketeering is a capital offense in the Soviet Union; it's probably more than that in the middle of Red Square—and handed over a pack of now-illicit spearmint.

"Do you have any more?" he wanted to know. Two more packs were offered, ten more rubles paid.

After this transaction I began to feel squeamish—people seemed to be looking at us now—so I took the fifteen rubles and rushed away to think about the new turn my life had taken.

Reflection, though, wasn't easy. As I walked back to the hotel, I attracted even more sidewalk entrepreneurs. I wasn't carrying any more packs of gum, but four of the dime pens went for five more rubles.

Safely ensconced in the Minsk Hotel, I assessed the situation. I could either reform and refuse to entertain the overtures of smiling Russian youths, or, in the capitalist tradition that is my heritage, I could make a killing peddling packs of gum and ballpoint pens.

As I said earlier, I'm not especially proud of the decision I made. Within forty-eight hours I was sold out of both gum and pens, and rolling in rubles.

Believe it or not, spending the newfound wealth in a relatively short length of time became something of a problem. The Soviets keep track of the foreign currency you exchange, and it's impossible to convert rubles into another money. The last day in Leningrad I ate four large meals, all with a serving of caviar, and made lavish gift purchases to get rid of the excess rubles.

Luckily, when I presented my financial declaration statement upon departure, the customs agent didn't inquire how it was possible to survive eleven days in the Soviet Union by converting only $10 into rubles.

Such are one's adventures in the gum trade. Now, with the Russians in the "chewing rubber" business, the Wrigley connection has been thwarted. Gone for latent criminals visiting the U.S.S.R. will be the exquisite temptation of receiving the equivalent of five dollars for a single pack of spearmint.

—*Washington Post*, April 5, 1977

Postscript

Writers remember firsts. The first byline. The first major article. The first essay using "I" that presents a tentative but personal voice.

This is the first op-ed newspaper column I ever wrote. Although dozens (scores, really) have followed, this one continues to occupy a special place in my memory. To have had it appear in the *Washington Post* seemed satisfaction enough at the time, but a few days later National Public Radio called to see whether I'd record an audio version for *All Things Considered*. Unfortunately, between the time of the producer's invitation and the taping, P. K. Wrigley, the top executive of the gum empire bearing his name, died. Somehow a lighthearted reminiscence titled "The End of the Wrigley Connection" struck me as bordering on bad taste, but the fellow at NPR didn't agree. "Don't worry," he responded. "We'll write around that. It'll be fine." As I listened to the package—an obituary and my contribution—I wasn't completely sure.

They're Everywhere

I own neither a power lawnmower nor a snowblower, and that dual deficiency raises a few eyebrows on my block. Neither do I process words, preferring to write with a trusty number 2 pencil. I am, I confess, so low-tech that the adjective "anachronistic" is insufficient; "antediluvian" is more like it.

There's a reason for my condition. Some people are handy, but I am (no other word fits) thumby.

The handy learn to master each modern machine as soon as it hits the market. The thumby never graduate beyond the self-service island at the gas station. For us, the label "maladroit" is cruel understatement.

Being thumby is a physical affliction that saps the spirit. It's the inability to hang a towel rack in the bathroom without jeopardizing one wall and the entire plumbing system. It's the hopelessness of attempting to replace a typewriter ribbon without looking like Al Jolson at the end. It's the determination to avoid buying any children's toy in a box bearing the phrase that's guaranteed to ruin Christmas Eve: "Partial Assembly Required."

Even though thumby people consider the phrase "modern convenience" to be a misnomer, that doesn't mean we object to inventions. I look at the majority of them admiringly, almost covetously, as products of progress, the objects that are taking us onward if not upward.

Up to a point, anyway. Some inventions aren't so much physically intimidating as intellectually objectionable. Billed as "creative advances," in reality they carry us backwards. Fortunately, telling the good from the bad involves mental rather than manual dexterity, and even someone with profound thumbiness can offer an errant observation or two.

A few years ago, when Sony brought its Walkman into this world, I gave thanks that people could listen to whatever they wanted in complete privacy. Those little earphones struck a blow for personal freedom and against noise pollution. What's more, the Walkman and its kin were easier to work than a standard tape recorder, a real advantage for some of us.

Lately, I've been having second thoughts. These gadgets now seem omnipresent and in constant use. The campus library at the university where I teach is such a popular place for them that if batteries were sold there, the profits would underwrite substantial new acquisitions.

The Walkman has strolled into the classroom, too. Some students religiously remove their headphones when a lecture starts and, just as religiously, reposition them the moment class ends. I've even seen students take exams to musical accompaniment. One, who had to be advised to lower the volume on his set, remarked after an exam, "I think better this way." His test score provided another opinion.

It's also common to see couples walking hand-in-hand around the campus lakes, each striding to his or her respective drummer.

That these machines mean so much to the young ought not to trouble someone slouching towards pedantry and a midlife crisis. But browsing in a local bookstore recently, I encountered a brand-new example of technology that provoked my wonder about where progress is taking us. It's a series of tapes that supply the plots, characters, themes, and historical contexts for classic works of literature. *The Odyssey, Hamlet, The Scarlet Letter,* and *Crime and Punishment* were among the titles on display; "additional titles are in preparation."

The promotional prose on each package is itself a minor masterpiece of Orwellian doublespeak. "Know the classics as you always wanted to," the potential purchaser is implored; "reacquaint yourself with the themes, deeper meanings, historical background and life of the author of the work." It doesn't take much wit to identify the target audience. I can't imagine Aunt Sally or Uncle Joe curling up in front of a fire to listen to a plot summary of *Crime and Punishment.*

Still, someone who utterly lacks technical aptitude probably shouldn't be firing spitballs at innovative folks exploring new territory in a free market.

What could be more American? Don't we all know that shortcuts are the roads most taken?

Nonetheless, I'm afraid I find these particular tapes both irritating and insulting. They claim to be "companions" to the classics. Not to put too fine a point on it, they're really acts of literary larceny which rob students of more than they may ever know. "Easy listening" now invades education, and a few minutes of tape time replaces hours of reading.

Mark Twain's *Adventures of Huckleberry Finn,* one of the titles in the tape rack, is one hundred years young this year. To celebrate the anniversary of this most American of classics, would it be too much to ask bookstore proprietors to banish that particular "cassette companion" from their shelves? Such a gesture might briefly interrupt the march of technology, but it would merit a grateful thumbs-up sign from a low-tech scribbler.

—Notre Dame Magazine, Autumn 1985

Postscript

The back page of *Notre Dame Magazine* is usually devoted to an offbeat, personal essay that serves as a "kicker" for an issue and tries to leave readers with something to smile or muse about.

This article is one such effort. In terms of personal aptitude, little has changed during the past two decades. The phrase "all thumbs" remains painfully self-descriptive. The Walkman phenomenon might be passé, both technologically and linguistically, but CD players, iPods, and other inventions are next-generation successors and now omnipresent on campuses and elsewhere. Plot summaries for great literary works also abound in audio and written formats. Such companions still keep students from wrestling with classic texts, making teachers pine for simpler times.

Reducing the Distance

For the first time since the semester began, each student in the class seemed engaged in the discussion. The academic ritual of raising hands before speaking had been abandoned shortly after the subject arose, and there was passion in their voices.

Three days earlier, the *South Bend Tribune* had published an article reporting that the dead body of a newborn baby had been discovered in a trash container of a dormitory bathroom at St. Mary's College. Located on the outskirts of South Bend, Indiana, St. Mary's is a Catholic women's school within walking distance of the University of Notre Dame—where the class in "Reporting the News" was taking place—and some journalists-to-be from St. Mary's were enrolled in the course.

The first story, a thorough sixteen-inch account, carried the name and home address of the student authorities thought had given birth to the baby. Subsequent stories in the *Tribune* (including one with the coroner's ruling that the infant had been born dead) also mentioned the name and address of the student, details not used by other newspapers or broadcast stations in the area.

No one in the class debated the newsworthiness of the story. Finding a corpse anywhere warrants attention and coverage. However, naming the woman—and continuing to do so—when no criminal charges had been filed was another matter, provoking a chorus of dissent.

As the discussion continued, one student, quite troubled by the possible consequences of printing the name, stated that rumors were circulating on the two campuses that some anti-abortionists were planning a protest at the girl's home in a nearby community.

"It's all because her name and address were in the paper," the student said. "Can't we do something to tell them what we think? How can we ask them why they did it?"

The student's questions and the class session as a whole dramatized what I consider to be a significant problem confronting the press in America today. Readers increasingly feel remote or distant from the newspapers in their cities, towns, and regions. People perceive the press to be large, impersonal institutions that deliver news, analysis, and commentary without bothering too much about public response or criticism.

One hears with growing frequency such statements as "the news media is too powerful" or "the news media is too arrogant." The use of singular verbs in sentences with "the news media" as the subject is not only sloppy syntax, but it also suggests (to me at least) that many people view "the news media" indiscriminately as a monolithic force far removed from people's lives and experiences. And the feeling of "bigness" breeds hostility.

In classes and outside talks, I try to explain that this perception of the press being remote is largely unfounded. Most news organizations welcome feedback from the public. At the very least a newspaper will publish corrections to its mistakes and letters to the editor taking issue with news coverage or editorial policies.

Yet, with the perception persisting, and (in my opinion) becoming more prevalent, I'm wondering whether the press might attempt to do even more to reduce this feeling of distance. Besides devoting space to corrections and to readers' letters, several newspapers in recent years have taken additional steps to establish more lines of communication with the public. Some of these measures include:

- publishing guest columns from readers that allow detailed responses to the handling of stories or particular editorial stances;
- establishing regularly scheduled and announced "talk with the editor" sessions, enabling readers to ask questions and register complaints either in person or over the telephone;

- appointing an ombudsman or reader's advocate to investigate concerns and problems that come from the public;
- distributing accuracy forms to news sources, asking whether stories were covered accurately and fairly;
- printing on a frequent basis a box or questionnaire with ample space for readers to provide their reactions to news reports and other aspects of the newspaper;
- organizing periodic open-forum discussions for the public, with these gatherings taking place in different parts of the community or circulation area and involving key personnel from the newspaper;
- devoting regular columns to the responses and explanations of editors and ombudsmen to questions and comments that come from readers or that arise internally in handling a story.

Speaking from experience, I know that many newspeople view some of these activities with suspicion. Some journalists think that what they do lacks general interest. It's shop talk, "inside baseball," without public relevance. Others dismiss "talk to the editor" sessions or open-forum discussions as acts of public relations devoid of much substance other than self-promotion.

I disagree. Handled appropriately, several of these activities can help to educate people about the press—its role and function, its procedures and processes, its strengths and weaknesses. With education comes understanding. There's less mystery about why a newspaper does what it does—or doesn't do.

Moreover, many of the measures mentioned engender a continual dialogue between the press and the public. Readers are less inclined to consider themselves as just a mass of people passively receiving information from a remote, impersonal organization. Having different avenues of access—that are taken seriously by the press—can help people to feel more actively involved, more engaged in what their newspapers deliver to them.

Activities that enhance education, dialogue, and access are diverse (as news institutions themselves are diverse), and at the present time they operate on several levels of accomplishment. What's needed in the future, I believe, is effective nurturing and development of such activities by the news media across the country.

If people perceive that measures like these matter, that they really count in the life of a news institution, then it's only natural that the public will feel less distant from the press. I would also hope that fewer people would have to ask: "Can't we do something to tell them what we think?"

—*Editor & Publisher,* October 25, 1986

Postscript

Since this article appeared, criticism of journalism has grown and recently become a staple of what one reads on the Internet or hears on radio talk programs. Mainstream news sources are doing more to create stronger connections with citizens, as the higher profile of ombudsmen or public editors at publications and broadcast outlets demonstrate. Despite such measures, instances of journalistic malfeasance—story fabrication, plagiarism, questionable sourcing, and the like—now receive more attention than in the past, undercutting institutional trust and credibility.

Finding ways of "reducing the distance" is one component in addressing the news media's problems. Emphasizing ethics and standards in the processes of newsgathering—the time before a story is printed or produced—will help prevent problems from ever developing. Just as undue speed causes driving accidents, the principle also pertains to journalism. Accelerating the news cycle in an effort to be first can, ultimately, result in dangerous situations or damaging consequences—for a particular medium and the media in general.

May 1970

"Did you hear that a bunch of students got shot?" a classmate asked as he rushed up to the makeshift stage near the flagpole on the Main Quad. "It just happened at Kent State. Some got killed."

The news triggered shock and disbelief among those of us milling around in the early afternoon sunshine, waiting for another antiwar rally to begin. Yet even before word spread about the Kent State violence, the demonstration planned on the campus at Notre Dame gave promise of being different from all the earlier ones.

Five days before, on April 30, 1970, President Richard Nixon had announced that U.S. troops were involved in an "incursion"—his word—in Cambodia. Instead of keeping his pledge to reduce American participation in the Vietnam War, the president was expanding the fighting that had been dragging on since the 1964 Gulf of Tonkin Resolution.

Campuses across the country erupted after Cambodia as never before or since. ROTC buildings at some thirty schools were burned during the week following the incursion. By May 4, the day of the Kent State shootings, students were striking at a hundred colleges and universities, and nearly 350 schools were soon to follow suit. At Notre Dame, word was out that a call to boycott classes would highlight this afternoon's rally.

The first speaker, however, told the crowd of almost two thousand something else. Reading from pages the wind kept lifting from the lectern, he said, "Striking classes as some universities are doing—in the sense of cutting off your education—is the worst thing you could do at this time, since your education and your growth in competence are what the world needs most if the leadership of the future is going to be better than the leadership of the past and present." Then, departing from his prepared remarks, he added, "We are living in an age of midgets. I want you to prepare to be giants."

The speaker, Rev. Theodore M. Hesburgh, C.S.C., was in his eighteenth year as president of Notre Dame. Although he argued against a strike, he struck a chord with many students and faculty that day by proposing a six-point "declaration" which called, among other measures, for "the withdrawal of our military forces at the earliest moment" and a commitment "to help work for a better America and a better world in a peaceful and non-violent manner." Hesburgh told the crowd if others supported his statement, he'd send signed copies to President Nixon.

Next, Student Body President Dave Krashna took the stage to advocate a more extreme course of action: he urged students to "stop, look, and listen—and absolutely say 'stop' to the education we're getting at this time." His call to strike had an immediate impact: attendance was sparse at late Monday classes, and more than half the student body boycotted classes on Tuesday.

From both the composition of the rally's audience and the response to the two speakers, you could feel the campus climate changing. Many people at Notre Dame who had shown no previous interest in doing anything to oppose the war now looked at Cambodia and Kent State with dismay.

Over the preceding four years, opinion about the Vietnam War at the university had been decidedly mixed. While growing numbers of faculty and students stood against the American involvement in Indochina and wanted a rapid end to the fighting, a large percentage supported U.S. policy and what it was trying to achieve, and a fair number had no strong views either way. The events of May enlarged the ranks of those opposed to the war—in just a few days, many in the mainstream center found common cause with those in the antiwar left.

Earlier that academic year, in the autumn of 1969, there had been a large antiwar march and Mass, but it was a solemn, one-day expression. Later in the fall, 250 protesters demonstrated against the Dow Chemical Company and the Central Intelligence Agency, leading to the suspension of ten students. But that autumn incident had an "us versus them" quality, whereas in May a spirit of solidarity quickly developed. Enough was enough. From this point on, opposition to the war became the majority point of view among students, faculty, and administrators.

The change of climate had repercussions throughout the University. Rev. John E. Walsh, C.S.C., vice president of academic affairs, formally suspended Wednesday classes. Thursday was the Feast of the Ascension, a traditional university holiday at the time. In his statement, Walsh quoted a resolution passed by the Student Life Council, an elected body of students, faculty, and administrators, asking the Notre Dame community to "set aside Wednesday and Thursday . . . as days for speeches, teach-ins and liturgical ceremonies to express the deep feelings and reservations about our government's recent actions in Indochina." Sanctioning the resolution, he said, was the university's response "to a widespread campus consensus."

As events continued to unfold, work on what became known as the "Hesburgh Declaration" and pressure from the strike activists converged. The passions and actions of those opposed to the war began to flow in the same direction. Yet despite the newfound unity of purpose, those who continued to support the war and those who opposed a strike still had chances to express their views.

I was struck by the seriousness, urgency, and intensity that pervaded the campus. Admittedly, my perspective was different from that of most students: I was working as the Notre Dame correspondent for the Associated Press and the *Chicago Sun-Times*. I had covered so many demonstrations and acts of student unrest that they tended to blur in my memory, then and now.

But what was taking place now was a far cry from what had been taking place at Notre Dame just prior to Cambodia and Kent State. Three days before the May 4 rally on the quad, thirty to forty students invaded the Center for Continuing Education, searched out the room where the university's board of trustees was holding its spring meeting, and pounded on the doors, forcing the trustees to cut the meeting short. In late April, about a thousand Notre Dame students held a panty raid at Saint Mary's College that had turned destructive: property damage and thefts added up to a $3,000 price tag.

Looking back at that time, which he calls his most difficult as president, Hesburgh says his course "was a monumental case of improvisation." He didn't know what might occur, and he carried in his billfold a list of the college and university presidents he knew personally who were driven from office or who died as a result of physical ailments exacerbated by the turmoil on their campuses. The number approached two hundred.

Hesburgh identifies the Cambodian incursion as the turning point in his own thinking about the war. "In my mind I was turning a very wide corner," he says. "It was high time to say, 'Get out now, tonight before midnight.'" He admits, though, that he had no idea what impact, if any, his rally speech and six-point declaration would have.

"It had been a horrible weekend," he recalls, describing the shouting and door-pounding at the trustees' meeting. "I got back to the Main Building about midnight on Sunday. I thought, if I had any brains I'd go to bed; but not having any brains, I went up to my office. A couple of kids came up and said, 'There's going to be a real blow-up tomorrow and you better be ready for it.'"

More students stopped by his office—one reporting a rumor that the ROTC building was going to be firebombed. Another told Hesburgh he might be asked to speak at the rally on Monday. "About 3 o'clock, Dave Krashna called to ask if I would talk. I said okay, and I thought I'd better have this one in writing, which I generally don't do."

Hesburgh remembers giving the talk "with whatever fervor I had," then walking to the barbershop in Badin Hall for a haircut. "When I went back to the office, there were a bunch of young people standing around wanting copies of the talk. I said, 'Sure, how many do you want?' They said, 'Thousands.' I said, 'What do you want all of the copies for?' They said, 'We're going to have students go to every house in town and try to have them sign the program.' I said, 'I'll tell you what: You guys do that and when you get all of the signatures I'll make sure the president gets them.'"

During the next few days there was not only a mood of seriousness but an explosion of energy. Students fanned out through South Bend and Mishawaka seeking signatures for the Hesburgh Declaration. Letter-writing campaigns churned out thousands of antiwar missives to the president, members of Congress, American bishops, and newspapers across the country. Discussion groups gathered each morning for what in the sixties were called "teach-ins"—or, more barbarously, "rap sessions." Students debated America's proper role in the world and prayed for an end to violence at home and abroad.

A mimeographed newsletter, the "Notre Dame Daily Striker," began appearing to compete with the *Observer*, which in the estimation of some strike leaders was not vigorous enough in supporting the campus turmoil.

Besides these ongoing efforts, special events—speeches, masses, marches, meetings—brought together large groups of students, faculty, and staff members. New York congressman Allard K. Lowenstein, the 1970 Senior Class Fellow and an early opponent of the Vietnam War, came to Notre Dame the day after Kent State and told an overflow crowd in Washington Hall, "We are grieved and wounded, but we are tough and ready to fight." Less than a week later, Indiana senator Vance Hartke urged a campus audience to "continue to protest the war by all peaceful means."

May 6 and 7—the Wednesday of suspended classes and Ascension Thursday—were pivotal days in Notre Dame's response to the turmoil. On Wednesday, more than a thousand people took part in a Mass on the Main Quad. While this was happening, a special faculty meeting was taking place in Washington Hall. After two and a half hours of robust debate, a resolution supporting the Hesburgh Declaration was passed 217 to 134.

Late that afternoon the largest march in the history of the University took place. Upwards of five thousand people, by official estimates, wound through the campus, then trekked through city streets to Howard Park near the Saint Joseph River for a community-wide rally.

On Ascension Thursday, thirty priests concelebrated a memorial Mass for the students killed at Kent State. That evening, with Friday classes looming, students supporting a continuation of the strike called an "emergency" meeting at Stepan Center. (The words "emergency" and "meeting" were frequently paired in those days.)

Trying to keep track of the arguments and counter-arguments, the motions and counter-motions at the meeting was almost impossible. The standing-room-only crowd witnessed little more than chaos. Finally, at the end of the session and amid considerable confusion, 1,309 students voted to continue the strike until May 15, another full week; 1,013 wanted to delay a decision until Sunday, May 10; 250 students favored ending the strike right then.

Walking away from Stepan Center, I remember thinking that the unity of the past four days was beginning to evaporate. Although strike activities involved well over a thousand students, some had started to question the ultimate value of a longer interruption of the semester. Classes were scheduled to end May 26.

After calling the Associated Press bureau in Indianapolis with a report of the student meeting, I went to a late-evening discussion about the war and related matters in the chapel of Saint Edward's Hall, where I lived. (Most halls conducted such sessions during this week.) My mind soon strayed from the speaker's words and locked on one he hadn't uttered: compromise. There must be a way, I thought to myself, to work out an agreement so that striking students could carry out their activities without infringing on the education and political views of other students.

Throughout that week the newspapers were full of stories about schools closing their doors and shortening the semester by as much as six weeks—reports many of us found dismaying. Such acts seemed starkly negative responses that, in essence, said "no" to both education and to the antiwar efforts of students.

The notion of trying to create a compromise appealed to other students in Saint Ed's. Inexperienced as we were—not one of us had any position in campus government or in the strike activities—we set out to draft a statement that would stake out a middle ground. As much as anything, we wanted to avoid identification with either the more radical or the more conservative groups. We sought acceptance, either hearty or grudging, from students, faculty, and administrators.

Writing the proposal took most of the night. As birds began to chirp outside the fourth-floor window, we had a three-hundred-word document modestly titled "Strike—A Consideration." The statement supported students who wanted to complete their semester courses; for the strikers, we outlined several options, depending on the type of course (required or elective) and the extent of involvement in, as the sheet put it, "activities in the spirit of the strike." In addition, we proposed to set up a series of not-for-credit courses to be offered by regular faculty members that in some way addressed the issues of the moment.

Not knowing exactly what to do with this plan, we decided to present it in the form of a petition that students and faculty could sign—everybody else seemed to be doing it; why couldn't we? Somehow, during the next three days, we collected more than six thousand names, going dorm room to dorm room and office to office.

During the weekend, we learned that Father Hesburgh had called "an emergency meeting" of the Academic Council, a policy-making body of administrators and faculty, for Monday afternoon. The meeting was prompted by the absence of large numbers of students from classrooms on Friday and the continuing intensity of campus concern. Over five hundred students on Friday alone had gone door to door in South Bend soliciting signatures on the Hesburgh Declaration.

Nine students were asked to talk for two to three minutes about strike activities past and planned at the Academic Council meeting. I was allotted four minutes to explain what, now less modestly, we were calling the "Academic Alternative Proposal."

Standing there in front of the council in the Center for Continuing Education, I expected butterflies to emerge from my mouth when I opened it. Being a participant instead of an observer felt unnatural. Halting delivery notwithstanding, I summarized the plan, emphasizing such words as "positive," "reasonable," "moderate." The last sentence steered to the middle course of the compromise and tried—however naïvely—to foster broad appeal.

When the council went into executive session, students waiting outside the room speculated about the outcome. A week earlier, Hesburgh had spoken out against a strike, and the day before he had reiterated his opposition on a CBS News special report. In the broadcast, though, he acknowledged that many students had just experienced "the most striking week of their lives"—presumably with no pun intended.

Late in the afternoon, the university formally announced measures similar to the compromise proposals. Noting that it would be "academically irresponsible" to suspend more classes, the council declared that "students participating in organized activities" who were not on scholastic probation could discontinue classes if they wished. Faculty members would determine final grades either by assigning the student's current grade, giving a pass or fail mark, or assigning a W (for withdrawal) or an I (for incomplete). The council also voted to excuse all class absences from May 4 to 11.

The compromise had worked. Flushed with success, the students at Saint Ed's started signing up professors to lead the "informal classes" we had proposed. Scheduling multiple sessions on such short notice quickly turned into a nightmare—as anyone with an ounce of sense should have realized—but individual meetings ("Literary Attitudes Toward War," "What Can a Physicist Do?" "History of Communist Involvement in Vietnam," "Successful Withdrawal of De Gaulle from Algeria") flourished in dormitories and elsewhere. After a week of upheaval, the campus settled into a new rhythm, a new equilibrium, that lasted for the final weeks of the term.

Putting those eight days of May in perspective now, Hesburgh sees the period not only as a personal turning point but as a fulcrum in Notre Dame history. "It was an enormous involvement of students in what was really a social movement," he says. "That was a unique and new thing."

So it was. The earliest manifestation of an antiwar effort at the university was a "teach-in" five years earlier, in the fall of 1965. In 1967 and '68, fewer than two hundred students and faculty demonstrated against Dow Chemical, ROTC, and the CIA. Those occasions always seemed to involve the same people, a reporter could observe. It was 1969 before Notre Dame began to reflect the mounting opposition to the war that had become so visible across the country.

In March of '69, the first Senior Class Fellow—an award formerly called "Patriot of the Year"—was Minnesota senator Eugene McCarthy, who had run for president in 1968 as a peace candidate. His visit that March was followed in the fall of '69 by a Mass on the library mall that included the burning of six draft cards—those of four students, one Notre Dame professor, and one faculty member from Saint Mary's—at the Offertory. An estimated 2,500 people took part in that Mass and a march to the ROTC building.

Shortly thereafter, 250 students protested recruitment activities by the CIA and Dow Chemical Company, the maker of napalm used in Vietnam, at the Placement Bureau in the Main Building. This confrontational demonstration resulted in the first and only use of the Hesburgh fifteen-minute rule, which had been promulgated the preceding February, not long after a conference on pornography and censorship that included police confiscation of a film. The fifteen-minute rule spelled out the consequences of campus disruptions in a 2,500-word letter to students and faculty.

In that letter, which was widely reprinted in newspapers and magazines, Hesburgh recognized "the validity of protest in our day—sometimes even the necessity." However, he also did what other academic administrators had been reluctant to do: he established a definite time limit for actions that violated the rights of other people or obstructed the life of the university. As he said in the document's most often quoted passage, ". . . anyone or any group that substitutes force for rational persuasion, be it violent or nonviolent, will be given 15 minutes of meditation to cease and desist." Even President Nixon applauded.

At the Dow and CIA demonstration in November, ten students tested the rule after receiving a warning that suspension or expulsion would result. All were suspended for one semester.

Looking back, Hesburgh sees a connection between May 1970 and his fifteen-minute rule. "What happened in '70 was the real turning point, but the letter had laid down the ground rules," he notes. "People were hungry for someone to stand up to the mob and say, 'Okay, this is far enough. We don't go any farther.'

"There had been some pretty rough stuff going on [at other schools]. The one thing that struck me, though, was that our students were different from the others in several aspects. They had an instinctive moral approach; it wasn't just the revolution for the sake of revolution. They really knew that there was a moral dimension to America. I think it's fair to say it's the first time in the history of this country that the young people educated and turned around the older people. It's always been the other way around. They were so convinced, and they were so universally worked up on this.

"The second thing that was important," he adds, "is that whenever we had a real crisis it was almost always tied to the liturgy. Many of our big moments during that terrible period were punctuated by masses at midnight out on the Main Quad."

"The third thing, I think, was that our students were never all that devious. We had a devious small group trying to really cause mischief—maybe not in their own minds; I don't want to judge them. They probably had high motives, as all revolutionaries do. But we also had a good, solid core of people who could be convinced otherwise. You could reason with them. If you gave them a decent program that responded to their idealism, they would pick it up and run with it. I didn't insist that they go all over town [with the six-point plan]; they did that on their own."

As it turned out, students collected twenty-three thousand signatures supporting the Hesburgh Declaration. In a letter to President Nixon accompanying the petition Hesburgh, who was then chairman of the U.S. Commission on Civil Rights, noted, "I have seen a moral rebirth on this campus during the past 10 days of May that is unparalleled in my lifetime, most of which has been spent at universities, mainly this one."

He received no response from the White House, and to this day doesn't know if Nixon ever saw his letter or knew about the petition. But the result of the public outcry across the nation, together with strong congressional disapproval, was a withdrawal of U.S. troops from Cambodia by the end of June.

After May 1970, a much different political mood reigned at Notre Dame. Dissent was less divisive. Questioning the war as well as its domestic fallout became more acceptable. Thomas Shaffer, now the Robert and Marion Short Professor of Law and from 1971 to 1975 the dean of the Law School, views what happened twenty years ago as the culmination of an evolving opposition to the war.

"The old 'God, Country and Notre Dame' patriotism had been in place in the mid-1960s," Shaffer explains. "Most people around here—at least most faculty members and I suspect most students—reacted as Notre Dame had always reacted to this country's wars, which was to support them. Then you had a period of that patriotic resolve gradually eroding. After 1970, Notre Dame was, by and large, a place of protest against the war, heavily because of Father Hesburgh's leadership—but he, too, had changed his mind."

The new atmosphere at Notre Dame went beyond opposition to the war, according to Shaffer. He subsequently saw more concern for issues related to social justice, to poverty law, and to peace studies across the campus. "There was a kind of maturation," he says about May 1970. "There then followed a period of heightened social concern."

Notre Dame *was* a different institution after what happened that spring. A few days after the rally in the Main Quad, I filed a dispatch to Associated Press in New York. A statement by one student leaps off the yellowing Western Union page today—not only as a personal comment but as a representative reaction to that time like no other:

"Up until Monday, I was sure I wanted to be a chemistry major. Then I found out that a friend of mine had been one of the ones killed at Kent State. I started attending the discussions and teach-ins, and now I'm pretty much convinced that I'll switch my major to something where I'll later have personal contact with people and not science equipment. With everything that's happened, it's probably a minor decision, but for me it's the most important thing I can do."

—*Notre Dame Magazine*, Winter 1990

Postscript

When students today inquire how earlier college days differ from theirs, I usually explain that the late 1960s were unprecedented and unpredictable— and that, in fact, two of my four undergraduate years ended early because of student upheaval. My sophomore year (1967–68) was spent in France, and to have lived in Europe throughout the spring of '68 meant you were a witness to widespread anarchy and daily demands for corrective change. Whole countries interrupted business as usual, with university-level classes just one area affected.

Two springs later, American campuses ignited, as both the war in Vietnam and antiwar opposition at home escalated. This article was written to coincide with the twentieth anniversary of an eventful time. The personal involvement described was—and is—very much out of character. The thinking behind it, however, remains curiously consistent.

Exactly thirty years after that spring of 1970, I published a book, titled *Indecent Liberties*. Its thesis ("gravamen" might be a more accurate word) is that Americans have a penchant for going to extremes in most aspects of life. The book's last sentence makes a final pitch for reasoned moderation: "America's future health and standing demand that each of us become something of an equilibrist, as we collectively do a balancing act and search for a center—of creativity and civility—that holds and endures." Exercising our freedoms often makes the seeking of equilibrium more difficult—but no less necessary.

The Grim Subject of Humor

Studying humor has never been a side-splitting, thigh-slapping experience. As I've told classes for a decade, E. B. White said it best when he remarked: "Humor can be dissected, as a frog can, but the thing dies in the process and the innards are discouraging to any but the pure scientific mind."

Not long ago, though, there was laughter in the classroom as we unscientifically dissected American humor. A Mark Twain novel, some examples of ethnic humor, a story by James Thurber evoked knowing snickers and even some hearty laughs.

No more. Like so much else these days, teaching humor has become a suspicious activity in this Age of Sensitivity.

Whole forests have been sacrificed to provide newsprint for articles describing the pros and cons of political correctness on campuses. The so-called PC movement is the academic answer to wider cultural concerns surrounding issues of race, sex, ethnicity, religion, and class roiling America in the 1990s.

None but a troglodyte could fire spitballs at efforts to enhance human dignity. And righting wrongs to achieve greater equality of opportunity is no laughing matter; it's an admirable national goal.

What I see, though, is a growing reluctance to respond to humor in the public setting of a classroom out of fear that any exercise of one's funny bone will be misinterpreted. To laugh with Mark Twain at some of the shenanigans of Huckleberry Finn and Nigger Jim might be disrespectful of a former slave and his people. To be amused at the number of people from a specific ethnic group it takes to change a light bulb might be offensive to members of whatever group is named. And so on.

It used to be different. Students seemed willing to accept that humor, by its nature, usually comes at someone's expense. A punch line had its own force—of provoking laughter or thought, approval or disapproval. Today it's stony, solemn silence, a hesitancy even to discuss the motivation behind a joke or the stereotyping involved.

This unwillingness to respond to humor is more a sign of the times than a suggestion that young people today are a humorless lot. Where I teach isn't a hotbed of the PC movement, but the chilling effect coming from the widespread politically correct thinking does freeze public reaction.

Nationally, in fact, some schools now have codes banning "inappropriately directed laughter" and the telling of certain kinds of jokes.

Outside the classroom it's another story. Away from a formal setting, many students find the likes of Eddie Murphy, Andrew Dice Clay, and Sam Kinison uproariously funny. These comedians build their acts on outrageous outbursts.

With routines revolving around women, minorities, gays, new immigrants, the homeless, and the handicapped, such performers are the furthest thing from hypersensitive politically correct thinking and expression.

Students today are caught in a crossfire of competing cultural movements. One force (principally the academic establishment) pulls them in the direction of sensitivity. The other force (largely popular culture) jerks them toward the shocking or sensational. There's no middle ground.

A teacher comes to understand the silence and sidelong glances in the classroom. It's risky to laugh if sensitivities might be violated. But privately—back in dorm rooms listening to tapes, or at movie theaters or comedy clubs—what's outlandishly crude or questionable, or both, becomes not only a source of entertainment but research material for academic essays.

Last semester, when a student handed in his major project of the term, he proudly said, "I liked doing that paper more than any other I've done, but don't show it around." It was about Andrew Dice Clay.

In 1990, Clay's *The Day the Laughter Died* became the first best-selling double-record comedy album in history. It is aptly named because the mean-spiritedness and unrelenting tone of hatred directed at some people overwhelm any sense of playfulness. I am not amused, saying so in class. But students writing about Clay admonished me for being so out of touch, miles away from the cutting edge.

Don't ask me to resolve the conflict between this public avowal of sensitivity and the private acceptance of the shocking. I can only hope that what's happening on either extreme subsides soon, with American culture returning to a common ground of understanding, tolerance—and laughter.

Until then, I fear, teaching humor will be as enjoyable as a root canal. No kidding.

—*Chicago Tribune,* November 14, 1991

Postscript

The night this column came out the phone rang at home while I was reading in bed. Twin brothers from a Chicago suburb—or so they introduced themselves—were calling to try to cheer me up. From the rather disjointed words of consolation, a cup or two of their own cheer might have preceded their hunt to talk with the writer of a sobering assessment of a subject they thought should be funny. "It must be a rough time for you," said one early in the conversation, but I restrained myself from laughing. Some minutes later, with the main thrust of their double-barreled solicitude clear, I thanked them for calling and hung up, shaking my head at such reader reaction.

I've never summoned the courage to offer another class about "American Humor." Students today tend to see contemporary performing practitioners as their models for understanding the subject, while I favor the written-word high jinks of Mark Twain, Finley Peter Dunne, Robert Benchley, James Thurber, or Peter DeVries. We're talking about bridging more than a generation gap to find out who gets the first—or last—laugh.

Being There

Coming from daylight into the darkened grandeur of Notre Dame Cathedral in Paris, I had trouble seeing. When I focused, it was on a picture of a statue of Mary and the Christ child, and then I realized I was seeing the image on a television screen. Moments later, I noticed TV monitors stretching all the way down the aisle of the massive church.

I couldn't believe my eyes. There amid the ambiance of awe-provoking antiquity and the jostling of hundreds of worshipers flocking to Easter Sunday Mass, television sets lined both sides of the nearly thousand-year-old cathedral. They were on carts positioned every several feet, next to the towering Gothic columns.

Elbowing our way forward, my wife and I found a place to stand near the altar, right next to one of the TVs and in line with one of the camera operators.

When Mass began, I confess I became absorbed in watching the monitor near us and contemplating television's presence in this setting. The incongruity of the modern machine in the venerable cathedral was jarring. Is nothing scared, I mused—or at least safe from the intrusion of television?

Such questions become even more nagging when one contemplates what lies ahead. Everywhere we turn these days we're hounded by accounts of the oncoming "information highway," as it's grandly called. In every medium, we are lectured about the video wonders just around the corner: five hundred channels, interactive communication, home shopping and banking, and—ultimately—the capability of personally programming whatever we want to see whenever we want to see it. *Time* magazine has already christened this future "the postchannel world."

To be truthful, fascinating as it might be to look down this fiber-optic, computerized road, I'm still having trouble coming to terms with the here and now, especially the many different uses of television today. During the 1992 presidential campaign, candidates kept popping up on programs that normally traffic in manifestations of abnormal psychology, or in "infomercial" settings favored by purveyors of kitchen products. Having Mass televised in Notre Dame Cathedral seemed just as unsettling.

Semester after semester, I tell my students that television changes whatever it touches. For good or ill, the presence of the most dominant medium of our times alters how people act and even how they see what's being broadcast. I point out that the reality of experience itself can change if the camera's point of view becomes our own. When perception and reality dance together, it's hard to tell which one's leading.

Yet as the Mass continued last Easter Sunday in Paris, the gloom of my reservations lightened as I realized that the production, befitting the occasion, had such dignity to it. There were no quick cuts. There were enough camera angles to capture what was happening. To add to the formality, the production crew even sported black ties.

During the sermon, as my broken comprehension of spoken French faded completely, I thought to myself: What does "being there" mean these days?

The most one can say is that the phrase continually takes on new meaning as new uses emerge for television. It's no longer merely a matter of "being there" by sitting at home and watching an event take place far away.

Now it's possible to "be there" by "being there"—to be personally present at an event while still keeping an eye on television's rendering of it.

As paradoxical or even profane as it might sound, for the faithful in the back of Notre Dame Cathedral struggling to see, or for the fans at any number of American sports complexes cursed with bad seats, television does enhance the experience of "being there." The actual and the vicarious converge.

Television seems simple to understand, because what it airs is often simplistic and because it is so much a part of our lives. But in reality, the medium is increasingly complicated and deserves sustained, discriminating attention.

A mini-epiphany on Easter about another role for television brings its own small reward. Yet I know only too well, it won't hold a candle to what we'll need to cope with the heavy traffic on the information highway when it begins to run to our homes. Stay tuned—or, as French broadcasters say, *"Restez avec nous."*

—*Notre Dame Magazine,* Summer 1993, and, with
revisions, *Chicago Tribune,* April 1, 1994

Postscript

Looking back, I wonder whatever happened to the much ballyhooed "information highway" we heard so much about in the mid-1990s. Did its many lanes merge with the ever-expanding Internet and the mushrooming world of satellite radio to take us into a communications jungle, where we're very much alone and on our own to find the messages we want or think we need?

Certainly the concept of "being there" assumes new meaning with increasing regularity. So-called "reality" programming on television takes us places we'd never go, and several examples of this genre raise a more basic question: Why on earth does anyone want to watch such fare?

Yes, television continues to change whatever it touches. Decades ago, the refrain of radio announcers was the plea, "Don't touch that dial." More and more, the impulse is to keep clicking a TV's remote control to try to discover what "being there" should really mean.

Scout's Honor

The consequences of political campaigns on candidates are frequently revealing. Running in a setting resembling a media-lit gauntlet provides lessons—both positive and negative—that citizens can use in forming their
opinions.

Until the other day, my opinion of Colonel Oliver North was (I confess)
not particularly high. In fact, not long ago while commenting on the Virginia
Senate race on this very page, I wrote, "A specialist in abnormal political psy-
chology could do greater justice to North, but suffice it to say that the Iran-
Contra miscreant comes to electoral prominence because the Republican
Party is splintering from factionalism and contempt for Congress is high."

The statement's pitch was deliberately high, but some not-so-gentle readers questioned the fairness of this analytical outburst and other similarly
barbed lines that followed. Didn't you go too far? they inquired.

Although some might still think so, I happily report that North himself
must not share this view. The mail last week brought a letter from the candidate, announcing his "No. 1 reason" for writing was his desire for this independent (and, I like to think, "balanced") correspondent to serve on his
"campaign advisory board."

Needless to say, the epistle—complete with two pennies glued at the top
of the first page—came as a surprise. He said he was sending his "two cents,"
and he wanted mine in return. The value of the advice flowing both direc-

tions strikes me as depressingly low, even a tad insulting. However, I was willing to suspend judgment for the sake of reading beyond the attention-getting gimmick.

What, you might ask, are the specific benefits and duties of joining North's advisory board? Well, the first seems somewhat premature. It's an invitation to a "pre-inauguration party." According to North, "I'll be sure to compile a photo album of the festivities and keep it for years to come. And every time someone comes to my office to visit me, they can thumb through that photo album and share in our spectacular celebration."

If attending isn't possible, I can send my own picture to enhance the album and still receive "an invitation beautiful enough to frame and hang on your living room wall to show all your friends and family." A member also gets "a special, embossed advisory board card," tangible proof (as North notes) for "family and friends that you're an important member of my campaign team."

Of much greater value from my pundit's perspective is "a special, confidential, unlisted telephone number (only for advisory board members) so you can call and give me your advice during the campaign. But you have to promise not to give the number to anyone else. Scout's honor."

Having someone everybody knows openly lied to Congress invoke "Scout's honor" might seem a presumptuous stretch. Be that as it may, he goes on to dangle a secret, "extra-special benefit" that he thinks advisory board members "will love" to cinch his side of the deal.

Whatever could it be?

Perhaps it's a picture of his principal opponent, Charles Robb (who's never named and merely referred to as "Lyndon Johnson's liberal son-in-law"), in a compromising position. Maybe it's the disclosure of his clandestine plan to serve as a self-proclaimed spy behind enemy lines, should he be elected to the Senate. One's imagination does roam.

After several paragraphs of appealing for money to meet the challenge from "every Sandinista-loving, far-left liberal special interest group," the colonel gave me pause and, truth be told, made me feel proudly humble. He said that "when the bullets start coming, it's important who's in the foxhole with you. That person can give you the support, encouragement and cover you need to survive and win. The person I want in my foxhole this election is you."

A stirring sentiment, to be sure. Yet given my earlier effusions about North, I really wonder whether he wants this sprawling physique and serendipitous psyche there with him in his foxhole. Has the take-no-prisoners battle of the campaign made him so broad-minded—liberal dare I say—that he's willing to let bygones be bygones, to forgive and forget?

At first I frankly didn't know what to do. The phrase "strange bedfellows" doesn't do justice to the situation. However, let's be fair: from this invitation, it's clear North has the courage to change and the bravery to welcome a wayward soul to his flock.

I'm returning North's two cents today, and accepting his invitation for the advisory board. I won't send a picture for the album, but I pledge not to reveal the special, unlisted phone number when he sends it to me. Scout's honor.

—*Chicago Tribune*, October 23, 1994

Postscript

Feuding within the Virginia Republican Party prevented Oliver North from winning a Senate seat in the momentous midterm elections of 1994. While, nationally, the GOP faithful celebrated achieving majorities in both the U.S. Senate and House of Representatives (in the House for the first time in forty years), North narrowly lost to incumbent Democrat Charles Robb largely because another Republican, Marshall Coleman, ran as an independent and received the endorsement of Virginia's senior senator, John Warner, a Republican.

North, however, did not fade into silent obscurity. With the current revolving door between electoral politics and media participation, he parlayed his celebrity into airwave and authorial success. Curiously, I never received the official documents certifying my place on his advisory board. The papers might be lost in the mail—or he could be waiting to make a posthumous appointment.

An Allergy to Abstraction

With Pavlovian predictability, every school year begins the same way. Religiously (albeit somewhat reluctantly), I stop by the philosophy department at the university where I teach to pick up a booklet describing courses for the fall term.

No, I don't have the slightest intention of enrolling in any classes. It's a matter of guilt.

For over a decade, I've had this nagging, at times gnawing, anxiety. Why—an inner voice keeps inquiring—do you persist at being blissfully ignorant of a subject vital to all learning? When (nudges this conscience-like tormentor) will you, who endured years of graduate school to be called a doctor of philosophy, take time to ponder verities leading to true understanding and knowledge?

Such questions, I confess, provoke the visits to this academic *terra incognita*. The course descriptions in undergraduate-accessible prose summarize the work of philosophers and list books a rounded, and grounded, person should study. As I know too well from my shaming internal reminder, behind Plato's chestnut that "the life which is unexamined is not worth living" is the four-square implication that philosophy provides *the* path to an examined, worthy state of being.

The names never change: Plato, Aristotle, Bacon, Descartes, Locke, Hume, Kant, Kierkegaard, Nietzsche, Heidegger. Titles, too, recur with disheartening consistency—*The Republic, The Nicomachean Ethics, Meditations on First Philosophy, A Treatise of Human Nature, Critique of Pure Reason, Either/Or, Beyond Good and Evil.*

Over the years haunting bookshops, I've picked up copies of these books and several others. They sit carefully arranged on a shelf not far from where I write and work up classes on, I admit, concrete (some might even claim pedestrian) subjects. Unfortunately, though, these books don't just sit there. They seem to stare back, as if to say, "What on earth are we doing here?"

In each case, underlinings, even fugitive *pensées* of one kind or another, litter the first few pages. The rest of the book, though, remains inviolate, page after page unread, unappreciated. No spine—literally or figuratively—broken.

And there, I fear, lies the problem, the crux of this matter of guilt. Good intentions always seem to founder on rocks of reality, sinking any hopes of sailing through works charting a more philosophically ballasted future.

This ill-fated voyage leads to a grudging discovery. The world of epistemology and phenomenology, of ontology and teleology, of empiricism and theism, and whatever (as Bob Dole might say) isn't for everyone. For some people suffering from a congenital curse psychologists no doubt have identified and unpronounceably named, Spinoza and Schopenhauer are soporific.

Boring isn't the *mot juste* for a mere layperson to use, but it comes mighty close. As the late E. B. White, America's laureate of common sense and clear writing, once observed, "It takes more than genius to keep me reading a book."

My burdened conscience received modest consolation the other day when I began reading an essay by Joan Didion. Explaining "Why I Write," she remarked: "I am not in the least an intellectual, which is not to say that when I hear the word 'intellectual' I reach for my gun, but only to say that I do not think in abstracts."

Yes, exactly. Dealing with "abstracts"—very much in the plural—is the root of the problem, my mind's Achilles' heel. I thought back to my saintly math teacher freshman year of college, himself something of a philosopher in approach and presentation. He talked frequently (and somewhat mysteriously) about the lines he drew on the blackboard "going off into infinity."

What does that have to do with anything? I wondered then, now some thirty years ago. The abstraction of it all proved so upsetting I was lucky to pass the course. And I remain perplexed today. Why worry about an imaginary black hole for blackboard figures?

Didion takes a similar tangent, recalling her own undergraduate attempt to explore "the world of ideas." She notes: "In short I tried to think. I failed. My attention veered inexorably back to the specific, to the tangible, to what was generally considered, by everyone I knew then and for that matter have known since, the peripheral. I would try to contemplate the Hegelian dialectic and would find myself concentrating instead on a flowering pear tree outside my window and the particular way the petals fell on my floor."

Being interested in "the peripheral" might, alas, also be my fate. However, there's a troubling finality to this view, as dead as those petals on the floor.

So we have recurring angst and those walks down the hall to the philosophy department. Fool's errand though it might be, there's a pull of intellectual obligation, the call of mental duty. Maybe, just maybe, appreciating philosophical abstraction comes with age. The old saw about education being wasted on the young does reveal a partial truth. Could it be, in essence, a matter of time?

You never know. At the flattering yet probably misguided urging of an author-acquaintance, I recently shipped a new book (about that least metaphysical of subjects: contemporary politics) and other literary confections to an agent in New York. Before too many visions of blockbuster deals disturbed my daydreams, he called.

"I don't think there's a large, popular market for what you do," he said. "It's much too philosophical." He repeated the word "philosophical" four more times in a conversation lasting a couple of minutes. A busy man had little time for someone with so pointed a head. "Know thyself" seemed to be his principal message.

Curiously, though, this curt, real-world rejection struck me as an unexpected compliment. Philosophical, indeed. One of these days I am going to sit down and master the wisdom of the ages. Perhaps next summer.

—*Philadelphia Inquirer*, September 2, 1996

Postscript

"The fascination of what's difficult" (in the words of a Yeats line) never seems to flag, but my allergy to the abstraction of abstruse prose persists. Not long after this essay appeared, I decided to end the charade of acquiring reading lists for books destined to remain unread. Self-knowledge takes time and (the wisdom of literary agents notwithstanding) often teaches lessons a person would prefer not to know.

Confessions of a Quote Slut

As the 2000 presidential campaign moves from the shadowy foreplay of pre-race fundraising into the limelight of media absorption, journalists will try to make sense of the unfolding spectacle by not only covering the candidates but by dialing the phone. On the receiving end of these calls will be members of a far-flung chorus of academic commentators offering their quick take on a day's story.

Serious though the work can be, it's not to be confused with the exactitude of any branch of political science. Everything from express-service punditry in the buff (one call during the 1996 campaign summoned me from a shower) to full-dress interviews that never appear become the lot of someone whose name ends up in the collective Rolodex of American journalism.

In the book *All's Fair*, James Carville refers to sources regularly contacted by reporters as "Quote Sluts." This label might offend many of the usual suspects in the dial-a-quote trade as unduly disparaging and dismissive. But, truth be known, I've been called worse, and more than a few practitioners of short-order commentary do, indeed, pant at the prospect of offering observations that reach beyond a seminar room or lecture hall. Some even sport beepers and mobile phones when electioneering heats up.

What's the seduction for anyone to be a quote slut? Although journalists often summarize a breaking news story and ask what-does-it-all-mean questions when their sources don't have a clue about the details or possible consequences, the work (as someone once remarked of the vice presidency) requires no heavy lifting.

In fact, more commonly a point uttered for contemporary relevance in a class or talk ends up being sharpened and recycled (for a wider audience) during such interviews. Fugitive perceptions that would never cohere into an article or column find their way into print, offering a sense of bemused satisfaction. Thanks to usually out-of-the-blue inquiries, these thoughts live on in cyber eternity for LexisNexis searchers everywhere.

Then there's the matter of ego. Vanity is an objectionable but absorbing vice. If you think you might have something to say for the betterment of the republic, it's difficult to decline a chance to opine on the passing parade. Duty calls.

My adventures in the quote trade began in earnest earlier this decade when I cobbled together several essays into a little book that carried the subtitle *American Political Life in the Age of Personality*. After *Harper's* magazine described me somewhat ostentatiously as an academic "who specializes in the country's peculiar fascination with personality politics," I fielded several calls from reporters, with each conversation starting with a line like, "I understand your area of expertise is personality politics."

Being a source, though, involves more than one-way trafficking in telephonic interpretation. For anyone distant from the daily chatter of Washington and its obsession with all things political, interviews can be as instructive for the interviewee as they can be helpful, at least potentially, to a reporter.

Stories and, yes, gossip from the campaign trail help a stay-at-home academic better understand and evaluate internal dynamics of a candidate's organization. What often goes unreported as "inside baseball" to the public at large is valued intelligence for a cloistered connoisseur of the political arts. Early whispers about staff disarray surrounding Bob Dole four years ago foreshadowed what turned out to be a lackluster campaign for the Republican nominee.

Moreover, many calls provide enduring lessons about the vagaries of journalism—what becomes news and what doesn't. My checkered if not plaid past includes one instance in which an Associated Press reporter called on a Sunday about a long-range piece she was doing about Vice President Al Gore's role in the 1996 presidential campaign. At the end of her planned questions, she inquired offhandedly: "While I've got you on the line, do you have any comment on what Ross Perot said today?" Thoughtful former students from hither and yon dispatched clippings from the next day's newspapers, complete with my top-of-the-head musings about the tall-tale aroma of the Texan's talk.

Earlier the same campaign year, three different reporters for that wire service called from Washington in the span of a couple of hours on one day. Not having spoken to anyone in the bureau for several weeks, I asked the third caller: "Is this my shift? Have you got a blackboard out there with people to call today?"

"No," he laughed. "We're not as sophisticated as that. You're on one of our lists, and it just happens that way sometimes."

With random selection and survival of the pithiest, it's impossible to know what, if anything, might happen after a source hangs up the phone. You learn, for instance, the importance of the angle a reporter is pursuing. Not following the predetermined angle can jeopardize the use of observations that take a different tack.

To confess: I've been serious when the interviewer sought sarcastic, and deliberately (or, at least, allegedly) amusing instead of pipe-smoking academic another time. In neither case did I know the slant the story would take, and in neither case did anything I said ever appear. My news analysis wasn't fit to print because it didn't conform to the planned approach.

These experiences, of course, raise questions about whether a reporter is trolling for a particular statement to enforce his or her viewpoint. When journalism veers toward ventriloquism, the source becomes something of a dummy, mouthing only what's wanted by a newsperson.

And on one occasion during the 1996 presidential campaign, I was the victim of what justifiably might be termed "interview *interruptus*." Dole had given a speech in Los Angeles about the entertainment industry. A Washington reporter called, seeking precisely three sentences of interpretation.

At the end of the second sentence, I heard some background commotion and a couple of choice expletives. "I'm afraid we won't be needing you," the reporter explained. "Editors have decided the L.A. bureau will do the react story."

Serving as a source means being on-call for the odd, occasionally offbeat request. A week before the 1992 presidential election, with some polls indicating a tightening race, a weekly newsmagazine tracked me down on a trip to conduct a lengthy interview based on the premise of why I thought George Bush had come from behind to win his second term.

This how-it-happened, hypothetical commentary featured definite verbs in the past tense and region-by-region assessments of the remarkable Bush recovery and triumph. Of course, with the lead time involved and the objective of being prepared for whatever occurred, the magazine was assembling interpretation "on spec." Actual results would ultimately dictate final copy. Given my train of thought, I never left the station: nary a word ever appeared.

Besides becoming acutely aware of the chanciness and contingency of journalism, someone in the source game learns the media practice their own form of incest. A reference one place often leads to others elsewhere. *USA Today*, for instance, is used as a daily tip-sheet for radio talk-show producers throughout America. A remark of one or two lines in that paper can lead to a flurry of requests to discuss the subject more fully.

The syndicated columnist and television commentator Mark Shields once likened a professional political analyst to a Christmas tree salesman. Frenetic, seasonal activity comes to a screeching halt on a definite day. The same holds true in the quote business. A week or so after an election, the volume of calls drops to the point where you almost long to hear from a telemarketer.

However, the advent of what's aptly called the permanent campaign in governing now means the telephone rings at other times as well. Monica Lewinsky's explosive emergence in 1998 sparked a five-alarm scramble among the usually sedentary band of armchair analysts. As the investigation began amid a cacophony of allegations, call after call sought speculation about the possible consequences of presidential hanky-panky—and worse. Would the president be forced to resign? Were these grounds for impeachment?

One incident remains memorable in that year of pontificating on matters mostly profane. The day of President Clinton's 1998 State of the Union address (less than a week after the news broke about the alleged Lewinsky affair) the *Dallas Morning News* carried a couple of my lines in its advance story. I'd jotted them down the day before in case of an inquiry. (For certain occasions a source prepares to be spontaneous.) Harking back to 1997, when the verdict in O. J. Simpson's civil case arrived exactly at the same time as the State of the Union speech, I remarked: "Last year Bill Clinton was competing against O. J. Simpson for public attention. This year he's competing against himself."

Other newspapers picked up the *Morning News* quote, and ABC Radio tracked me down in a Chicago hotel (where I was getting ready for a post-mortem program about the speech) to have me say it on tape. Late that evening, cruising through the TV channels back at the hotel, CNN began a speech story with the now well-traveled comment. Stunned by this newspaper-radio-television trifecta, I felt trapped in a multimedia echo chamber.

Today, with the 2000 presidential campaign taking shape and gathering momentum, the unpredictable world of quote sluts and sources will begin to spin with unscholarly speed. For just the fifth time in the past half century, an incumbent president won't be competing, adding that variable to the electoral calculus.

Will Gore overcome his prominently played early problems or face a bloodying challenge from fellow Democrat Bill Bradley? Will talk of George W. Bush's past persist and provide traction for Republicans Elizabeth Dole, Steve Forbes, or John McCain? Will Jesse Ventura and the Reform Party muscle their way to the campaign's center stage? Who knows?

Yet there's one abiding certainty to the uncertain calling of the quote trade. Being a source means never having to say "no comment."

—*American Journalism Review*, October 1999

Postscript

For several months after this essay appeared, calls seemed fewer than before, a possible sign of paranoid guilt or the bruised sensitivities of certain reporters who recognized themselves in the assembled anecdotes. Of late, pundit traffic seems about normal, and I continue to profit (in understanding politics and journalism) from the exchanges.

I have learned, though, that reporters do respect responses admitting an absence of knowledge almost as much as a quotable utterance. One correspondent phoned with some regularity about a subject largely foreign to my experience or expertise. During the fourth call, I confessed considerable ignorance in what he was asking about. "That's okay," he replied with a small laugh. "It's always informed ignorance." Those last two words, "informed ignorance," might be appropriate to include on my tombstone.

Lost and Found

DUBLIN, Ireland—When the invitation to dine at the residence of America's ambassador to Ireland arrived the other day, my wife and I considered it a pre–St. Patrick's Day stroke of good luck. I looked forward to peeking behind the curtain of Irish-American relations.

Early the morning of the dinner, we booked a cab for 7 p.m., emphasizing the need to be at the ambassador's in Phoenix Park by 7:30. Calls at 7:05 and 7:15 brought keep-your-shirt-on responses. At 7:20, when the cab appeared, the driver said he'd do what he could to make up the time, complaining about the growing frustration with Dublin's rush-hour conditions in recent years.

Entering Phoenix Park, Europe's largest and double the size of New York's Central Park, the cab driver slowed down when passing the Wellington Monument and mentioned a herd of deer roam free across the nearly two thousand acres of land. At a "roundabout" intersection along Chesterfield Avenue, he stopped, pointing out that one gated lane led to the American ambassador's and the other to the state residence of the president of Ireland.

In the darkness, we saw little—but the symbolism was easy to read. Ireland's strong ties to the U.S. extend to where the country's president and America's highest representative live. Theirs are the only residences in Phoenix Park.

At 7:40—and already ten minutes late—the cab driver gave our name to the guard at the gate, who briskly checked us off his list. A uniformed military aide greeted us at the door, took our coats, and asked us to sign the guest book, saying, "You're not that late. Another couple is expected."

Ushered into a drawing room, we couldn't pick out the ambassador, Michael Sullivan, who's much involved in the intractable Northern Ireland peace process. Immediately, the thought crossed my mind that the former governor of Wyoming might be conducting hush-hush business elsewhere.

The only face in the small crowd we did recognize belonged to none other than Mary McAleese, the president of Ireland, whom by chance we'd met a week earlier after a lecture she'd given at University College Dublin. With her in attendance, I wondered about others on the ambassador's guest list.

Leaving people with whom she was talking, she came over to say hello. We visited a few minutes, and she then excused herself for presidential mingling.

Moments later and after drinks were served, President McAleese returned, asking if we'd been in the house before. I confessed it was the first time we'd visited Phoenix Park, but reported the cab driver made a point of stopping to show us the entrance to her residence.

"Come with me," she said, fully expecting her to show us around in the ambassador's absence. Finding one door locked, she tried another, leading to the now-empty hall.

"I didn't want anyone in there to hear this, but I'm afraid there's been a mistake," she said with a sensitivity uncommon in the corridors of power. "You're in the wrong place."

In an instant, the mystery of the missing ambassador was solved. With the opposite of four-leaf clover luck, we had unwittingly crashed a function at Áras an Uachtaráin, this country's White House. The ambassador had been notified two errant Americans were assaulting the hors d'oeuvres at another party, and a car was dispatched to right the wrong.

With indigenous Irish charm, President McAleese encouraged us to return to the reception while the social—and political—*faux pas* got "sorted out"—a favorite, all-purpose phrase here for dealing with life's vagaries.

Stupefied, even speechless, we rejoined the group, now suspicious the looks from others as much as inquired, "Who are those people taking up so much of the president's time?"

To call our entrance at the ambassador's a dramatic one would be only partially correct. There was, however, much head shaking and laughter as we met others who'd been told about our undiplomatic detour.

At the end of the evening, when the ambassador from Mexico offered a ride home, we immediately accepted, thinking it much less chancy than calling a cab.

What do you write in a letter of apology to the president of a country after crashing an official party? Even for someone who spends part of each day trying to string words together, the best I could muster invoked Ring Lardner's crack about "Gullible's Travels" and a groveling thank-you for kindness to such strange strangers.

But I followed up by doing what only seemed right. We sent the president of Ireland the nicest St. Patrick's Day card I could find.

—*Chicago Tribune*, March 17, 2000

Postscript

Since this column was published, I've discussed it in classes about journalism as an example of a writer's innocence—or obliviousness—to the impact of words and to their varied meanings, depending on the reader. Composing the piece, I wanted to emphasize the theme of an innocent abroad and to praise the cordiality of the Irish head of state. Pegging it to run on St. Patrick's Day observed journalistic topicality. What could be less controversial than these straightforward intentions?

Unfortunately, the president's staff viewed the whole situation differently and reacted with alarm. Didn't I realize, a highly placed caller wanted to know, that I reported a "serious breach of security" and exposed to the public a private matter involving the president? Did I plan to tell the story to any Irish journalists?

It was not a conversation I anticipated, and I later learned official displeasure even made its way to the American ambassador. At a function in Dublin a few weeks later, he half-jokingly remarked: "You might be the first person deported on my watch."

For space reasons, the published column didn't include the following two paragraphs near the end:

> After Ambassador Sullivan briefly mentioned the arrival misadventure in his welcoming toast, an Irish woman across the table asked, "How could that have happened? You might be a terrorist."
>
> With the continuing "troubles" in the North, I understood her concern. Yet, given my age and physique, I also took the remark as a left-handed compliment.

You might conclude that the Irish woman was raising legitimate warning flags with her question and comment. I missed them—and immediately plunged forward with self-directed put-downs for comic effect.

Looking back, do I now regret putting pencil to paper to recount this experience? I really can't decide. All I know is that I do try harder to gauge the potential reaction of people I write about. Any such effort, though, remains an imperfect science, with snares and traps one might never see.

Obsession

So there we were, surrounded by the majestic natural splendors of Yellowstone Park, and I was getting jumpy, sorely in need of a fix.

For three days, a long holiday weekend, no newspapers penetrated our remote camp, and the picture-postcard mountains blocked reception of television or radio signals. Late the next day, finding a day-old issue of the *Billings Gazette* at a small general store was like discovering a Dead Sea Scroll. Close perusal revealed that little of consequence had happened since our last exposure to journalism, calming any out-of-the-loop anxiety.

At the dawn of the nineteenth century and to begin one of his memorable poems, William Wordsworth lamented, "The world is too much with us." Two hundred years later, with the Information Age at a full gallop, America still reeling from the 9/11 attacks, our troops in Afghanistan, the Middle East in turmoil, and domestic affairs in a state of unrest, "the world" captured by the news media is seemingly without end and (wilderness sojourns excepted) very much "with us."

It might sound anti-Wordsworthian, even somewhat anti-intellectual, but I revel in this new environment of easy access to disparate messages from modern technology. More choice means greater possibility for receiving additional reporting and analysis about a particular subject of import or interest.

One of Wordsworth's contemporaries, Charles Lamb, famously remarked, "Books think for me." Today books compete with other purveyors of words and images for both time and cerebral stimulation. Yet, with due diligence, a picture of how things are can emerge from connecting together bits of information from a variety of different sources.

Making this argument—like getting jittery about vacationing in a no-news climate—frequently makes my friends shake their heads. Why, for heaven's sake, do you spend so much time each day consorting with suspicious sources? How on earth can you bear to read five daily newspapers and religiously catch several television and radio programs?

Granted, questionable coverage of *some* recent stories (notably, a couple of notorious Hollywood murders and two scandalous sagas involving Washington interns) has made the media easy targets for stern criticism, elevating dissatisfaction and reducing confidence. Sixth-sense skepticism is appropriate not only for practitioners of journalism but also consumers of journalism.

Today's communications cornucopia lets each person decide. What publications or programs meet my specific concerns? Which ones seem wanting or even violate my sensibilities? In short, indiscriminate disapproval makes little sense amid the bounty of such diversity.

Ironically, audiences shrink as the media world explodes, a consequence of expanding choice. In this constantly changing milieu, a reader, viewer, or listener needs to be more active in selecting a properly balanced information diet.

As you might guess, on occasion I've been accused of something akin to hyperactivity in trying to keep up with the news. Insomnia has few redeeming consolations, but a bedside radio, equipped with a pillow-friendly earphone and tuned to reports from the BBC World Service, has become a nightly ritual in our household.

When Spiro Agnew died a few years ago, I judged the bulletin worth reporting to my slumbering wife at shortly after 3 A.M. Later that day, in a tough-love tone, she established her "Incumbent President Only" rule. From then on, any news of the passing of a former president, let alone a disgraced ex–vice president, could wait until her first cup of coffee.

"A good newspaper, I suppose, is a nation talking to itself," the playwright Arthur Miller once observed. Now, with so many voices competing for attention, it's increasingly difficult to establish the kind of dialogue Miller describes. But this doesn't mean the media, all of them, shouldn't try—and keep trying.

Whether or not they're successful, I (for richer or poorer) foresee no end to what some see as a strange necessity. The novel has aptly been called "the bright book of life," but reality—indeed, truth itself—is stranger than most fiction, a continuing puzzle to solve: piece by piece.

On the same trip west to explore Yellowstone, we stopped in Jackson, Wyoming, on a Sunday afternoon. By some mysterious providence, a copy of that day's *New York Times* appeared for sale in one of the shops. Although a cheapskate by nature (just ask aforementioned spouse), I decided that paying triple the usual cost was well worth the price.

—Notre Dame Magazine, Summer 2002

Postscript

As the mainstream news media desperately try to adapt to competition from attention-diverting alternative sources, it often seems they transport their shrinking audiences down-market with them. In the scramble for survival, quantity (the cold numbers of readers, viewers, or listeners and their demographic peculiarities) keeps getting confused with quality (the well-chosen words and images that illuminate a significant subject).

Fortunately, this new, message-abundant environment offers a citizen several options for seeking information of value amid the plenty of mediocrity. Increasingly, I find myself turning to agencies and outlets abroad for coverage of international affairs. Satellite and Internet technologies provide access portals, if we're willing to enter them.

Complaining about media performance offers emotional and psychological satisfaction. But constantly venting doesn't really serve a larger purpose. Seeking what's meaningful is something we have to do on our own in our own ways. As the common pool of information becomes more polluted with sensationalism, superficiality, and stupidity, we need to turn elsewhere—and to navigate new waters that lead to different landing points of understanding and knowledge.

A Look at the New World

If "The child is father of the man," as a line of Wordsworth's poetry proposes, it probably follows that the student is parent of the teacher. Solving the unending riddle of the classroom comes as much from the yesterdays of youth as today's technological wizardry. Memorable instructors provide models or novel approaches, while the environment for learning (what happens beyond a syllabus or curriculum) often inspires the stumbling first steps of independent inquiry.

Such ivy-covered rumination might help explain why someone takes to the road and becomes something of a nomad. Since 1997, I've taught away from my home institution on five separate occasions, but I trace this pedagogical itinerancy to my own, long-departed student days.

For an unworldly Hoosier boy, the prospect of going to Europe for ten months sounded romantic and adventurous. Back in the 1960s, the University of Notre Dame began to develop its first study-abroad programs—there are now some twenty possibilities—and the one based in Angers, France, started in 1966, the fall of my freshman year. So that semester I enrolled in a class with what you might call zero-based understanding of the French language. *Sans* an iota of previous instruction, I dreamily hoped I could conjugate enough verbs to spend sophomore year in France.

I'm now convinced a mother's prayers rather than linguistic mastery sent me across the Atlantic the following August. The word "callow" grossly understates how at least one eighteen-year-old felt during the initial weeks of innocence abroad.

To have lived in France at that time, particularly during the massive student and laborer protests of spring 1968, allowed an outsider to witness a country going through the throes of revolutionary change. Schools, including the university where we studied, closed. Workers struck. Postal and transportation systems stopped. Demonstrations, often bloody, abounded.

What was happening back home proved just as engrossing, as I learned the value of studying America from different vantage points. The assassinations of the Reverend Martin Luther King and Senator Robert Kennedy, the growing opposition to the Vietnam War, the violent racial unrest, and Lyndon Johnson's surprise decision not to seek re-election all received maximum attention abroad. The commentary raised searching questions about the stability and future of the United States.

For the first time, I read beyond the sports pages of newspapers and magazines. I developed the daily habit of picking up the *International Herald Tribune*. As I went through the pages, my youthful ambition of someday becoming a sportswriter began to fade.

What was occurring elsewhere at that tumultuous time constantly competed with the daily enchantments of a provincial French city. As I followed the swirling currents of events overseas, I started to finagle for ways to get closer to them.

Saint Augustine once wrote, "The world is a book and those who do not travel read only one page." The thinking behind that precept, I realize today, influenced trips on my own away from Angers: to Israel and its newly occupied (still controversial) territories, to Greece under the control of a military junta that had just seized power, and to the Soviet Union in some chillier days of the Cold War, among other places.

I now better understand that period's career-shaping consequences. In one of his countless quotable asides, G. K. Chesterton, a connoisseur of paradox, observed: "The whole object of travel is not to set foot on foreign land; it is at last to set foot on one's own country as a foreign land." To a degree, my student experience served that ironic purpose. Despite seductive diversions in journalism and politics, I finished graduate work in American literature and American studies, continuing all the while to remain fascinated by what the New World means to the rest of the world's peoples, cultures, political systems, businesses, and everything else.

After returning to Notre Dame in 1980 to join the faculty, I looked forward to a time when teaching off-campus might arise. Learning a new language or revivifying my moribund French seemed as remote as running a four-minute mile, but English-speaking assignments did present themselves.

In each case, I made sure to pack not only lecture notes for subjects to discuss but also blank notebooks for the random jottings that new activities and perceptions provoke. The teacher would also be a student, learning about another country and more about one's own in the process.

In a foreign clime, I discovered that the unexpected can be amusing, even telling. During an atypical cold spell at the University of Notre Dame Australia in Fremantle, I was surprised one morning to find several sun-accustomed young Aussies wearing gloves as they took notes. At University College Dublin, after encouraging more robust discussion among Irish graduate students about America's influence, each session lasted longer than the previous one, and, blessedly, there was no impatient fidgeting. In a seminar at Saint Augustine College of South Africa, I listened to passionate arguments from blacks and whites that journalists there should concentrate more on positive news to help build that country's fledgling, post-apartheid democracy rather than being preoccupied with coverage of social and political problems.

At one foreign post, a student expressed his cross-cultural shock at my Yankee severity by complaining to the dean that the visiting instructor actually seemed serious in demanding regular attendance. Beyond such classroom contretemps, extended sojourns elsewhere opened my eyes to distinctive traits of another culture and what they signify for life there.

In Australia, for instance, you hear repeated reference to "the tall poppy syndrome." This, I quickly learned, has no relevance to gardening. Down Under, the egalitarian ethos remains so strong that to stand out from everyone else raises eyebrows. The indigenous impulse to find out why someone is different takes the shape of public examination—often undertaken by media sleuthing. That process can, and usually does, reduce a person's standing, with the "poppy" returning to the relatively same level occupied by fellow Aussies.

In Ireland, it doesn't take long to realize that contemporary politics intertwines with history at almost every turn. The Easter Rising of 1916 is a key moment on the road to an independent Irish Free State, formed in 1921 and followed in 1949 with the creation of the Republic of Ireland. But the origins of the republican movement, with its goal of ending British sovereignty throughout the island, dates back to the eighteenth century—and, to be sure, Catholic/Protestant "troubles" took root a couple of hundred years earlier than that. To understand the current Northern Ireland peace process and general day-to-day political life in Ireland, a historical primer is as essential as a morning newspaper.

Outside the classroom, citizens of others countries are naturally eager to tell a visitor about their own domestic matters. Before long, however, the discussions evolve into questions (and opinions) about the United States. In today's globalized world, fascination abounds about our influence and dominance, especially in the realms of popular culture, economic involvement, and governmental policies.

Few conversations circumvent political matters. What's striking to a visitor is the fixation on the American presidency that exists abroad. The United States might be this time's sole acknowledged superpower, yet that status tends to get personalized by focusing on the occupant of the White House. It's as though there's a realization that our president's decisions will ultimately mean something—for better or for worse—to everyone beyond our borders.

During the later years of Bill Clinton's time in office, it was common to be interrogated in winking, wry ways about the relevance of his private appetites, leading to the more encompassing concern about whether Puritanism survives as the American creed for someone in public life. With George W. Bush, a certain quizzical fear about his administration's foreign policy has constantly competed with the broader fascination with the U.S. role in the world.

I was stunned by the question a South African woman stood up to ask in Johannesburg at a public lecture that took place even before the war in Iraq began. She wanted to know if I thought September 11 was "fortuitous" in permitting the president to pursue his international objectives.

By implying that the multiple tragedies of that September day could have been fortunate happenstance suggested a depth of worry and criticism I never expected—and tried, however vainly, to refute. As it turned out, though, her question proved more restrained than some of the pointedly scabrous queries that followed. It was an unsettling but instructive evening.

A year later, during the U.S. occupation in Iraq and while teaching at Notre Dame's London Centre, I was struck by the assessments about America one found in European sources. Books, magazines, and newspapers surveyed the subject from several angles, and the BBC World Service devoted a six-part radio documentary, *Age of Empire*, to the global reach and stature of the United States today.

The BBC series looked back at the emergence of America as an international power, but focused primarily on the nation's current unrivaled position economically, militarily, and culturally. Why, the correspondent kept wondering, is the U.S. "both admired and reviled, often at one and the same time"? Examining all these appraisals, I came to the conclusion that foreigners view us differently from how we see ourselves.

In his 2004 State of the Union address, President Bush repeated an assertion he had made in earlier speeches: "We have no desire to dominate, no ambitions of empire." Such statements notwithstanding, people abroad perceive an empire in fact (of daily commerce, cultural influence, political involvement, and military presence) that belies protestations to the contrary.

Explaining this "no, I'm not/yes, you are" phenomenon, the British historian Niall Ferguson, author of *Colossus: The Rise and Fall of the American Empire*, asserts: "Freud defined *denial* as a primitive psychological defense mechanism against trauma. Perhaps it was therefore inevitable that in the aftermath of the September 11 attacks, Americans would deny their country's imperial character more vehemently than ever. Yet as U.S. foreign policy has moved from the defense to the offense, the need for denial would seem to have diminished. It may thus be therapeutic to determine the precise nature of this empire—since empire it is, in all but name."

Another non-American observer, Michael Ignatieff, a Canadian without the U.S. prejudice frequently found in contemporary commentary, sees the situation in less starkly Freudian terms, arguing in *Empire Lite* that "Americans have had an empire since Teddy Roosevelt, yet persist in believing they do not." Like Ferguson, Ignatieff identifies a native reluctance to entertain imperial ideas. Developing his theme about the U.S., he notes: "It is an empire lite, hegemony without colonies. . . . It is an imperialism led by a people who remember that their country secured its independence by revolt against an empire, and who have often thought of their country as the friend of anti-imperial struggles everywhere. It is an empire, in other words, without consciousness of itself as such."

How foreigners, rightly or wrongly, react to what they interpret as Yankee imperialism covers a spectrum of response. Support, rejection, and bewilderment joust with each other whenever the subject comes up. Sometimes, however, a reaction can be worrying.

During office hours last spring, a Notre Dame student in the London program told me about a troubling recent occurrence. While reading by herself in a coffee shop, she sensed an older man at a nearby table watching her. As she looked up, he asked, "You American?" When she admitted her citizenship, he began yelling at her in an unknown tongue before storming out and abandoning a fresh cup of coffee. Now the object of everyone's attention, the student promptly departed, wondering what triggered his outburst. She'll never know—but also will never forget the incident.

Particularly with a foreign program, what happens away from the classroom can rival in educational benefit the more formal course work. In my own student days, I happened to be in Moscow when Robert Kennedy was assassinated in California during his presidential campaign.

At the Tass News Agency office, as I stood in front of several huge, black-and-white pictures of the New York senator sprawled out on the floor after the shooting, the man next to me inquired if I might be American. I nodded a yes. I remember his next question as though it were posed yesterday: "Why do you Americans kill the Kennedys?" His curiosity about national complicity—rather than the tangled webs of conspiracy theories—put the matter in a sobering, even disturbing perspective.

Near the end of my last overseas sojourn in London, I spent a rewarding Saturday morning touring the Chelsea home (with its soundproof writing study) of Thomas Carlyle, the nineteenth-century historian and essayist. My attention focused on an observation of his I stumbled upon: "What we become depends on what we read after all of the professors have finished with us. The greatest university of all is a collection of books."

Carlyle is right—but only up to a point. Continuing enlightenment also comes from immersing oneself in the surroundings and cultures of people other than ourselves. Recognizing this makes the world beyond our shores less foreign—and our understanding of America more acute. In addition, one would hope, it somehow helps the perennial student-traveler in trying to become a better teacher.

—*Notre Dame Magazine*, Winter 2005

Postscript

Venturing out beyond domestic tranquility with a fair amount of regularity puts the lie to Emerson's famous aphorism: "Traveling is a fool's paradise." One rarely discovers paradise, but—in an interconnected world where the U.S. plays a preeminent role—it is anything but a fool's errand.

The trick is to spend enough time in another country, and culture, to gain perspective about a particular place. Occasionally, such awareness can lead to a new understanding that also provides lessons about a person's homeland. The future is, of course, unknown, but we can get ready for it by learning as much as we can about our current time and world.